The Peace of God

PAST IMPERFECT

Past Imperfect presents concise critical overviews of the latest research by the world's leading scholars. Subjects cross the full range of fields in the period ca. 400—1500 CE which, in a European context, is known as the Middle Ages. Anyone interested in this period will be enthralled and enlightened by these overviews, written in provocative but accessible language. These affordable paperbacks prove that the era still retains a powerful resonance and impact throughout the world today.

Director and Editor-in-Chief

Simon Forde, *'s-Hertogenbosch*

Acquisitions Editors

Erin Dailey, *Leeds*
Ruth Kennedy, *Adelaide*

Production

Ruth Kennedy, *Adelaide*

Cover Design

Linda K. Judy, *Michigan*

The Peace of God

Geoffrey Koziol

ARC HUMANITIES PRESS

Library of Congress Cataloging in Publication Data

A catalogue record for this book is available from the Library of Congress.

© **2018, Arc Humanities Press, Leeds**

Printed and bound by CPI Group (UK) Ltd, Croydon, CR0 4YY

ISBN (print): 9781942401377
eISBN (PDF): 9781942401384
eISBN (EPUB): 9781942401391

arc-humanitiespress.org

Contents

For Annie,

瑤碧玉珠

Abbreviations

AASS	*Acta sanctorum quotquot toto orbe coluntur.* 68 vols. Antwerp: Société des Bollandistes, 1643–present. http://acta.chadwyck.com/.
Bessin	*Concilia Rotomagensis provinciae ...* Edited by Guillaume Bessin. Rouen, 1717.
CJS	Chartes originales antérieures à 1121 conservées en France, Centre de Médiévistique Jean Schneider, Université de Lorraine (Nancy). Traitement électronique des manuscrits et des archives (TELMA). http://www.cn-telma.fr/ originaux/index/.
Cluny	*Recueil des chartes de l'abbaye de Cluny.* Edited by Auguste Bernard and Alexandre Bruel. 6 vols. Paris, 1876–1903. Cartae Cluniacensis electronicae. http://www.uni-muenster.de/ Fruehmittelalter/Projekte/Cluny/CCE/.
Constitucions	*Les Constitucions de Pau i Treva de Catalunya (segles XI–XIII).* Edited by Gener Gonzalvo i Bou. Barcelona, 1994.
GEC	*Gesta episcoporum Cameracensium.* Edited by L. C. Bethmann. MGH SS 7:393–525.
HL	*Histoire générale de Languedoc.* Edited by C. Devic, J. Vaissète, et al. 16 vols. Toulouse: Édouard Privat, 1872–1904.

Mansi	*Sacrorum conciliorum nova amplissma collectio.* Edited by J. D. Mansi et al. 31 vols. Florence and Venice, 1759–98. http://www.documentacatholicaomnia.eu.
MGH	Monumenta Germania Historica. http://www.dmgh.de/.
	Capit.: *Capitularia regum Francorum.* Edited by A. Boretius and V. Krause. 2 vols. Hanover, 1883, 1897.
	Conc.: Concilia.
	Const.: Constitutiones et acta publica imperatorum et regum.
	Formulae: *Formulae Merowingici et Karolini Aevi.* Edited by K. Zeumer. Hanover, 1886.
	SS: Scriptores in folio.
	SRG: Scriptores rerum Germanicarum in usum scholarum separatim editi.
Newman	William Mendel Newman. *Catalogue des actes de Robert II, roi de France.* Paris: Sirey, 1937.
Orderic Vitalis	*The Ecclesiastical History of Orderic Vitalis.* Edited and translated by Marjorie Chibnall. 6 vols. Oxford: Clarendon Press, 1969–80.
Ordonnances	*Les Ordonnances des rois de France de la troisième race …* Edited by E. de Laurière et al. 21 vols. and supplement. Paris, 1723–1849.
Rodulfus Glaber	Rodulfus Glaber. *Historiae libri quinque.* Edited and translated by John France. Oxford: Clarendon Press, 1989.
PL	Patrologiae cursus completus … Series Latina. Edited by J.-P. Migne. 221 vols. Paris, 1844–1902. http://pld.chadwyck.com/.
RHF	*Recueil des historiens des Gaules et de la France.* Edited by M. Bouquet et al. 24 vols. Paris, 1869–80.
Saint-Maixent	*Chartes et documents pour servir à l'histoire de l'abbaye de Saint-Maixent.* Edited by Alfred Richard. Poitiers, 1886.

A Note on Sources

Given the number of Peace councils and decrees, it has not been possible to cite all the primary sources by which each is known. In any case, the citations are readily available. Goetz, "Kirchenschutz," gives complete references for the early ones. Hoffmann, *Gottesfriede*, both identifies the sources and provides considerable critical commentary. For the later Peace in southern France and Catalonia, see the citations in Bisson, "The Organized Peace," and Carraz, "Un *revival* de la paix?" The primary sources for the early German *Landfrieden* and *Reichsfrieden* are, for the most part, discussed in Wadle, *Landfrieden*.

A few Peace decrees have been translated into English in the appendices to *The Peace of God*, edited by Head and Landes, and in *Vengeance in Medieval Europe: A Reader*, edited by Daniel Lord Smail and Kelly Gibson (Toronto: University of Toronto Press, 2009). A few independent translations can also be found online.

Map 1. Important place-names for Chapters 1 and 2.

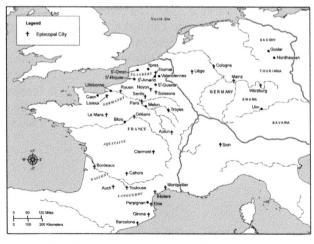

Map 2. Important place-names for Chapter 3.

Introduction

When the Apostle Paul wrote that "the peace of God ... surpasses all understanding" (Phil. 4:7), he did not have in mind the historical movement known as the "Peace of God." But he might as well have, for few subjects in medieval history have received so many contradictory interpretations. Many have believed that it was a response to a surge of violence among the aristocracy; just as many deny there was any surge of violence at all. Some think it was fundamentally a millenarian movement that marked the first appearance of "the common people" on the political stage; others think it was neither millenarian nor popular. It has been seen as a movement in which bishops wrested responsibility for maintaining social order from secular political leaders; as a movement used by secular political leaders to reassert their responsibility for social order; as a movement spearheaded by monks for the reform of society and the church. It has been thought one of the most transformative events of the Middle Ages. It has been thought a sideshow.

Given such disagreements, it is hard even to define exactly what the Peace of God was, since any definition requires one to take a stand on the above debates, at least implicitly. So for the moment one must keep to a very open definition. The Peace of God was a program originating in the last years of the tenth century that protected certain specified categories of persons and places from certain kinds of actions. Broadly speaking, the places protected were churches and their environs; the persons protected were the unarmed. Speaking even more broadly, the actions prohibited were the kinds that historians have tended to classify as "violence" of the sort habitually perpetrated by a warrior aristocracy. The movement began in southern France (specifically, in Aquitaine), soon took root in Burgundy, and from there spread widely: to Provence, Catalonia, Languedoc, and Septimania; to Normandy, Flanders, and the royal domain. Ultimately it even entered Germany, where it soon evolved into a slightly different institution known as the "territorial peace" or *Landfriede*. As it spread, its stipulations became more precise and new limitations were established. The most important of the new limitations prohibited nearly all acts of violence during specified periods of time—this being known as the Truce of God. Of course, the devil is in the details and the details are complicated. For that reason, it may be helpful to state, at the outset, some of the arguments that will be presented.

First, the Peace of God did rely on some traditional structures and injunctions inherited from the ninth-century Carolingian reform. Yet it was also something truly new and different. The only way scholars have been able to minimize its novelty is by cherry-picking evidence, thereby greatly oversimplifying Carolingian discourses and practices of peace. In order to explain this argument, in order to understand exactly what in the Peace was new and what was old, it will be necessary to deal somewhat extensively with the antecedents of the movement. This essential background is presented in the first chapter.

Turning to the second chapter, on the Peace and Truce themselves, there probably was no great increase in "violence" in the late tenth and early eleventh centuries. There was, however, an increasingly dense implantation of lordships. These lordships were not those of new castellans only. Bishops, cathedral chapters, and monasteries were also establishing more coherent lordships. As a result, there was more friction locally among those who had claims to lordship, creating the perception that violence was a greater problem than it had been. Also as a result, lords had a greater need to delimit their respective rights and powers where their powers bordered each other or were interspersed with each other. The Peace of God was one of the first and most fruitful means by which lords created the territorialization of local power that became a hallmark of the high Middle Ages.

As to why the Peace of God has been interpreted so differently by so many different historians, two reasons will be advanced. First, the movement changed as it entered different regions. The politics of the Auvergne, where the program first appeared, were not at all the same as those of Poitou, where it next appeared. When the movement was then adopted in Burgundy, Flanders, Normandy, and Catalonia, it came into regions whose politics were different yet again. Although a program with a very consistent set of stipulations, the Peace of God was adapted to many different political landscapes. Moreover, the sources that inform us about the specific instantiations of the Peace and Truce belong to a number of different genres. A conciliar decree, a chronicle, an episcopal *gesta*, a piece of hagiography, a charter, a circular letter, all had their own distinctive characteristics and concerns. As a result, each type of source reveals a different aspect of the Peace of God; none reveals it in its totality. In fact, the most seductively detailed sources may well be the most misleading of all.

Finally, the Peace of God did not end violence; it simply tried to establish measures to prevent it, while codifying when and where one could apply it if such measures failed.

Nevertheless, one can still maintain with some plausibility that the development of the Peace and Truce of God really was one of the most important events of the entire Middle Ages. For it was in articulating the program that secular and ecclesiastical leaders learned how to legislate in ways that overcame the limitations of what had passed for legislation under the Carolingians. And in implementing the program, they created the kinds of institutions that empowered local communities to govern themselves. This is the subject of the second and third chapters.

Chapter I

Before the Peace of God

According to the Gospel of John, peace was Christ's principal bequest to his apostles and through them to his church: "Peace I leave you, my peace I give you" (John 14:27). The context makes it clear that this peace was a tranquillity of the heart, not a peace of the world.[1] Yet as Augustine saw, the church was necessarily a political society, existing in the world even while waiting for it to end.[2] What, then, did the peace of God mean for the church on earth, a mixed community of saints and sinners?

There were two basic answers. One was a Stoic idea which was taken over by Neo-Platonists, from whom it was received by Augustine, who gave it its most famous formulation.

> The peace of the body consists in the duly proportioned arrangements of its parts. The peace of the irrational soul is the harmonious repose of the appetites, and that of the rational soul the harmony of knowledge and action. The peace of body and soul is the well-ordered and harmonious life and health of the living creature. Peace between man and God is the well-ordered obedience of faith to eternal law. Peace between man and man is well-ordered concord. Domestic peace is the well-ordered concord between those of the family who rule and those who obey. Civil peace is a similar concord among the citizens. The peace of the celestial city is the perfectly ordered and harmonious enjoyment

of God, and of one another in God. The peace of all things is the tranquility of order. Order is the distribution which allots things equal and unequal, each to its own place.[3]

This was a kind of Grand Unified Theory of peace. It brought together microcosm and macrocosm in a single whole, so that cosmology, political theory, and psychology all obeyed the same principle: in peace, the inferior willingly conformed itself to the superior. Throughout the entire history of the Middle Ages, no learned person would have disputed the truth of this formulation. On the other hand, simply because it was a Grand Unified Theory, Augustine's notion of peace was not particularly helpful in solving the problems of real life and so was not often explicitly discussed, even though it was nearly everywhere assumed.[4]

More important for theories and practices of peace in the Middle Ages was a central institution of Roman law: the pact (*pactio*). Historians often define a pact as an agreement between two or more autonomous parties acting of their own free will. In fact, the legal definition was somewhat more restricted: a pact was a stipulation willingly agreed to by two autonomous parties appurtenant to a legally recognized transaction between them. The law of pacts was already well-defined in the time of the Roman jurists Ulpian and Paul (*Digest* 2.14). Although the Theodosian Code devoted only a single brief chapter to them (2.9), this did not reflect their unimportance but the contrary, for parties were allowed to use pacts to establish any sort of agreement that was not against morals or the law and the agreement would be fully binding at law. Given their versatility, pacts appear to have been extremely common in Roman vulgar law (that is, the Roman law that was actually practiced in the provinces). Thus, they were fully approved by the *Lex Romana Visigothorum*—the early sixth-century compendium that became the most commonly cited source of Roman law during the early Middle Ages.[5] They also received the imprimatur of Isidore of Seville, in his *Etymologies* (5.24), the period's single most important source of basic knowledge. And sixth- and seventh-century formularies from the Merovingian kingdoms show pacts being used to establish a wide variety of binding agreements: for example, adoptions, settlements in cases of rape, divisions of property among heirs, and exchanges of property between landholders.[6]

Looking back with the benefit of 1,500 years of hindsight, the centrality of pacts to the political and legal life of the early Middle Ages seems overdetermined, meaning that a number of distinct factors reinforced a preference for pacts. First, pacts were versatile instruments that could accommodate many different situations at a time when law and society were changing rapidly. Second, in the Gallic provinces of the sixth century a circumstance had already developed that remained characteristic of the entire Middle Ages. There were many different sources and centres of power locally, regionally, and supraregionally. There were many different systems of law that might apply to any two litigants or any single object of litigation, including the different "personal laws" that applied to Salians, Ripuarians, Burgundians, Visigoths, and Romans, and the developing canons that applied to church property and clerics. Under these conditions, disputes were often ended—and potential disputes headed off—by the use of bilateral agreements freely entered into by the parties themselves, either on their own or through the mediation of friends, relatives, patrons, and the powerful. Perhaps most important of all in this rapidly Christianizing society, pacts were by definition a kind of peace. They therefore attracted to themselves an entire discourse of Christian love and organized it into a rich and vibrant discourse of Christian peace.

The Christianization of pacts was already well advanced in the earliest formularies, particularly for pacts associated with churches and those that regulated the division of inheritances between kinsfolk—for the love between brothers was already treated as emblematic of the spiritual love that should obtain among all Christians as sons of God. Already feuds were being ended by the intervention of "priests and great men" who negotiated pacts returning the antagonists "to the concord of peace." Already we find the idea that pacts replaced the coercive power of judges and judgements with agreements made between parties who acted "freely," "out of charity," and "for the good of peace."[7] Nowhere do we see these associations more clearly than in one of the first extant pieces of "legislation" from the new Merovingian dynasty, the *Pactus pro tenore pacis* ("Pact for the maintenance of peace"). This was an agreement made (perhaps) soon after 524 between the two Frankish kings Childebert I and Clothar I, sons of Clovis. The two brothers had separate but bordering kingdoms. Theft (especially cattle rustling) was rampant along the border, because thieves from one kingdom could enter the other kingdom, steal, and retreat back across the border to safety, and posses (*trustes*) from the victims' kingdom could not pursue the raiders across the border. The pact between the two kings ameliorated the situation by allowing posses to cross the border in pursuit of thieves. Significantly, although the *Pactus* contained separate stipulations regarding theft enunciated in the name of Childebert and Clothar individually regarding their own kingdoms, the stipulations that allowed cross-border entry between their kingdoms were enunciated as a joint statement issued in the name of both kings together. And only this stipulation was introduced with an express justification articulated in the vocabulary of Christian peace: "since by God's grace, the love of brotherhood keeps an unbroken bond between us."[8]

However, the fullest examples of Christian peace language in the early Middle Ages are found in the acts of episcopal councils from fifth- and early sixth-century Gaul. The bishops were the heirs of some 500 years of Christian rhetoric and sacramental theory built around the idea of peace as found in the Old and New Testaments, especially in I Corinthians and Ephesians.[9] Furthermore, the Gallic episcopacy was strongly collegial: one of its bedrock principles was that all bishops were spiritual brothers and therefore equals, making a language of "judgement" distasteful. And the tumultuous events of the fourth, fifth, and sixth centuries wreaked havoc with existing administrative boundaries, meaning that lines of jurisdiction were often unclear and subject to disagreement. For all these reasons, Gallic and early Frankish councils often formulated their most difficult decisions—particularly decisions involving bishops—in terms of a "love" that maintained "the unity of the Spirit in the bond of peace" (Eph. 4:3). The result was a profoundly coherent discourse of love, peace, and unity associated with collegial and consensual decision-making, to the point that bishops could speak of their synods as "our association of peace." The same language of peace, fraternal love, and concord was subsequently adopted by Frankish episcopal synods such as Tours (567) and Mâcon (585) for analogous situations whenever bishops needed to emphasize their equality and the uncoerced collegiality of decisions.[10]

An episcopal language of peace, love, brotherhood, consensus, and unanimity also found an important place elsewhere in western Europe—for example, in the great Toledan councils of Visigothic Spain and the English council of Hertford. On the other hand, given these bishops' somewhat different needs, they placed less emphasis on peace and love and more on unanimity and authority. The same was true in the last great Frankish councils whose acts are extant, Paris in 614 and Clichy in 626/27. Summoned by the strongest of all Merovingian kings, both councils emphasized royal commands, not episcopal collegiality, and the single canon from either council that explicitly mentioned peace envisioned it quite differently than early Gallic councils. This was a peace that benefited the king and the kingdom, a peace conjoined not to consensus but to punishment: "Let there be perpetual peace and order (*pax et disciplina)* in our kingdom with the favour of Christ, and let the rebellion and insolence of evil men be repressed most severely."[11]

Peace under the Carolingians

After Clichy progressively fewer councils were held in the Frankish kingdoms, and apparently none at all between 696 and 743. But with the Carolingians everything changed. The council or assembly became the single most important institution of government. It was no longer an episcopal council held under royal auspices but an assembly that brought together both secular and ecclesiastical elites into a collective, deliberative, consultative body. This was already true of the very first councils summoned by the authority of the Carolingians when they were still mayors of the palace. But the transformation was most marked in the general assemblies (*generalia placita*) held under Charlemagne that set the seal on his conquests and initiated the program often described as "the Carolingian reform."[12] The requirements of the program were often communicated in documents known as "capitularies," because they were presented as lists of articles (*capitula*). Among the most impressive of them was one of the very first, a collection of eighty articles known as the *Admonitio generalis*. The first fifty-nine provisions are a distillation of the canon law collection which Charlemagne had received from Pope Hadrian I (the *Dionysio-Hadriana*). Articles 60 through 80 are a contemporary redaction usually attributed to the Anglo-Saxon scholar and teacher Alcuin, whose eloquence and commitment to pastoral care are evident throughout. The first of these additional articles (c. 60) demands that bishops and priests read and preach the Catholic faith to all the people, for this is "the first command" of the Law: "Hear, O Israel, that the Lord your God is one God, and he shall be loved with all your heart and all your mind and all your soul and all your strength" (Mark 12:29–30; Matt. 22:36–38). The second (c. 61) introduces a formulation of peace unlike anything that had previously appeared on the continent.

> That there be peace and concord and unanimity among all the Christian people between bishops, abbots, counts, judges, and all everywhere, whether greater or lesser, since nothing is pleasing to God without peace, not even the gift of the holy offering at the altar, as we read in the Gospel, where the Lord himself commands it, for this is the second command in the Law: "You shall love your neighbor as yourself" (Mark 12:30; Matt. 22:39).[13]

In a sense, what Alcuin did was expand the ideals of the episcopal *conventus* to encompass all Christians of all statuses and orders. This is not to say that Augustine's idea of peace as an order of subjection was overthrown. Subsequent capitularies of Charlemagne and his bishops continued to call for "peace" and "love" between Christians as "equally the sons of Christ"; but they also strongly asserted the duty of inferiors to honour and obey superiors: children their parents, wives their husbands, monks their abbots, abbots and monks their bishop, and so forth.[14] Still, in a fundamentally important way, Alcuin's formulation (which in this respect was less like Augustine's than like Gregory the Great's) was radical in its forthright assertion of the equality of all Christian people. We will find the same duality in the Peace of God, not because the Peace used any writings of Alcuin as a source but because the duality was inherent in the medieval understanding of peace and society.

In any case, simply because it was grounded in the equality of all Christians regardless of rank or status, Alcuin's formulation had no long future before it. Its distinctive wording and values continued to appear in royal capitularies and conciliar acts from Charlemagne's reign, particularly the most probing, such as the four great councils Charlemagne summoned to meet simultaneously in 813.[15] But generally, it became more common to speak of "peace" in broad terms as a self-evident good in itself, not to be defined but to be mobilized as a slogan. Thus, one of Louis the Pious's capitularies stated that three obligations were especially to be respected: first, to defend, exalt, and honour the church; second and third, "to safeguard peace and justice among our entire people."[16] Justifying the *Ordinatio imperii* in 817, he spoke of the need to maintain "the security and peace everywhere conceded by God." Those who deposed Louis sixteen years later justified their actions by accusing the emperor of being "a creator of scandal and a disturber of the peace and a violator of oaths," because he had tried to overturn this same *Ordinatio*, which had been established "for the peace and unanimity of the empire and the tranquility of the church by the common counsel and consent of all his *fideles*."[17] Louis's son Charles the Bald, ruler of the West Frankish kingdom, claimed to rule "for the royal honor and the peace of the people committed to us," so that "this Christian people might have peace."[18] A bishop who supported Charles's elevation as king of Lotharingia in 869 offered prayers that as king he would "keep us in safety and peace and tranquility." On the same occasion a panegyrist praised Charles as "a peacemaker, like Solomon."[19]

So far as this rhetoric had any content, it lay in applying the Catholic Church's principle of unity to the empire while at the same time appropriating an old Roman imperial notion that only a strong ruler could bring security, justice, and order to his subjects.[20] Both developments tended to undermine Alcuin's idea that peace issued from the love of all Christians for each other in their eschatological equality, regardless of rank and status. Instead, "peace" was now often conjoined to "justice," as in the just mentioned capitulary of Louis the Pious. In such usages, "peace" was a condition of civil tranquillity and order created and maintained by the ruler for the benefit of a people who were powerless to defend themselves in the face of abuses of power. And since counts and bishops were "partakers in ministry" of the ruler, it was their special responsibility to protect the people from acts of injustice. As Louis admonished his counts in the 820s:

> It pertains especially to your ministry that you show reverence and honor to the holy church of God and live harmoniously with your bishops, and that you offer them aid in fulfilling their ministry so that you both do peace and justice in your ministries.[21]

In this way, Alcuin's formulation of peace that had encompassed all Christians was narrowed, as capitularies began to speak instead of "peace between bishops and counts." Indicative of the trend was a canon of the Council of Mainz in 847, which quoted a canon from the 813 Council of Mainz, which itself quoted Alcuin's statement of 789. But while adopting Alcuin's plea that there should be "peace and concord and unanimity among the Christian people," the 813 council omitted Alcuin's explicit statement that such peace encompassed all Christians "whether greater or lesser," while the 847 council added a qualification:

> Therefore, if there should be peace and concord among all the faithful ... how much more should it exist between bishops and counts, who rule the people of God after the

summit of the imperial dignity. So let them have concord between themselves, so that not only do they not undermine one another in executing the service of God and fulfilling their ministry but rather aid each other.[22]

A second notable development of mature Carolingian expressions of peace was the resurrection of the sort of pacts between kings that had appeared under the Merovingians, only now they were much more frequent, their language and rituals were much more deeply Christianized, and they were much more central to political events. Already in 806, in the act by which Charlemagne planned a division of his territories between his three sons, the emperor acted "for the sake of the peace that we desire shall perpetually endure between them." As an expression of this "peace" he prohibited the brothers from entering each others' kingdoms with hostile intent, demanding instead that they bring aid to each other.[23] Louis the Pious's *Ordinatio imperii* of 817 established his eldest son as emperor with his two younger brothers ruling under him as kings. This was done "for the benefit of the empire and to keep perpetual peace between them and for the protection of the entire church"; and every year the two younger brothers were to make a formal visit to their older brother, with gifts, in order to "discuss with brotherly love what pertains to common utility and perpetual peace."[24] After Louis's death and the outbreak of war between his sons, pacts of brotherhood (*fraternitas*) were consistently used to frame treaties between them. The same continued to be done by the sons' sons and grandsons. The *locus classicus* is the very first such agreement, the alliance established at Strasbourg between Charles the Bald and Louis the German in 842.[25] Thereafter, every alliance between Carolingian kings (whether brothers, nephews, or cousins) and every treaty ending a conflict between them was framed in similar terms—Meersen in

847 and 851, Valenciennes in 853, Koblenz in 860, Savon-
nières in 862, Tusey in 865, Metz in 867, and Furon in
878. The first meeting at Meersen, for example, brought
together Charles the Bald, Louis the German, and Lothar,
who jointly issued a series of articles "concerning peace
and concord and unanimity between the three brother
kings, that they be united by the bond of charity sincerely
and not feignedly and that no one shall sow any reason for
scandals between them." To that end they promised to aid
one another against the enemies of each, to preserve the
honour of the church in their individual kingdoms, to pro-
hibit plundering and unjust exactions (*rapinae et depraedationes*) in their kingdoms, and to appoint *missi* to hear
the complaints of the poor and make judgements "according to the equity of law."[26]

Whereas the above deployments of "peace" were common to the entire Carolingian empire, a few usages were
either distinct to the West Frankish kingdom or especially
pronounced there. Since the Peace of God originated in
that kingdom, these must be addressed. The first was
almost entirely peculiar to it: the idea that the leading
men of the kingdom might engage in a pact with each
other and with the king. Its earliest appearance came
in November 843, at a time when Charles the Bald des-
perately needed to shore up his support among his lay
leaders and mobilize that of his bishops. The result was
a capitulary issued at Coulaines that Peter Classen called
the "founding document of the west Frankish kingdom."
Among its most interesting traits, it specifically referred to
a meeting of Charles's magnates and prelates—the meeting being called a *conventus*—at which all met "as one"
for the sake of "love and fidelity." Together, they made an
agreement among themselves—a *convenientia*. This *convenientia* Charles ordered written down and subscribed
personally by everyone in attendance, *including* himself,

so that "under Christ, the one head, truly as one man within the body of one church, each one a member of the others, what profits all shall be spoken unanimously by all with one voice." This written agreement was described as "a pact" (*pactam*) made by "episcopal authority and the unanimity of the faithful" to support "our honour and royal power." According to its terms, the prelates and magnates promised to support the king. In turn, the king promised to maintain the privileges of the church and the clergy, and to maintain the honour and law of those faithful to him. This, Charles declared, was the "treaty of harmony" (*foedus concordiae*) into which he himself had entered and which he himself and all the others had subscribed "in order to maintain peace and charity." Anyone who acted as a "rebel" against the treaty would be warned "in Christian love" to "keep the bond of charity inviolate" so that he might be welcomed back into the "association" (*societas*). If he refused, bishops, kings, and magnates would combine to take suitable action against him.[27]

Strangely, the *societas* established at Coulaines was very like the one kind of "peace" the Carolingians consistently opposed: the *coniuratio* or "guild."[28] This was an association made between groups of individuals who confirmed their commitment to each other "by right hands" (*per dextras*) or by oath (*sacramentum*). Carolingian rulers consistently treated them as "conspiracies" (*conspirationes*) and prohibited them absolutely. According to an important capitulary of 802, if members of a *conspiratio* sealed by oaths did harm, those who actually did the harm were to be executed; other members of the association were to whip each other and cut off each other's noses.[29] Why the Carolingians punished such associations so harshly is not entirely self-evident. In part, it was because rebels might organize themselves as *coniurationes*. In fact, one capitulary explicitly spoke of "conjurations and

conspiracies of rebellion" made "against the king or ecclesiastical dignities or powers of the *res publica*." Their
members were said to undermine "peace and concord" by
sowing "discord and dissension."

> Whence we ordain ... that they shall be removed from
> the communion and consort of all Catholics who love true
> peace, and unless they incorporate themselves back within
> ecclesiastical peace by penance and amendment, we order
> that they be cast out by all sons of peace.[30]

Yet Carolingian rulers were well aware that rebels did not
need to form an explicit *coniuratio* in order to rebel. The
magnates who conspired against Charles the Bald in 858
had sworn loyalty to his brother Louis the German but evidently not to each other, for though called a *societas* they
were not accused of having formed a *coniuratio*.[31] It was
the *coniuratio* itself that the Carolingians opposed, as if
"associative" oaths were acts of rebellion in and of themselves. The only oaths they tolerated besides ordinary
judicial oaths were vertical oaths, as from Charlemagne's
reign on they insisted that oaths of loyalty could only be
sworn to the ruler or to one's own lord.[32] Oaths could not
be sworn to peers to form self-help organizations. Self-help
associations were permitted, at least under Charlemagne,
who allowed collective agreements (*convenentias*) for the
sake of mutual aid in cases of shipwreck and damage from
fire and for purposes of alms-giving; but he explicitly prohibited such agreements from being sworn associations
whose members took oaths to aid to each other. Other
evidence suggests that such self-help associations were
especially common along the northern sea coasts in order
to underwrite action against pirates and raiders.[33] The
very last West Frankish capitulary, issued at Ver by Carloman in 884, supports this surmise. It prohibited rural residents from forming any "association, which in the vernacular they call 'guild' (*geldam*), against those who rob and

plunder them." Instead of forming a guild, when faced with such troubles residents were to inform the priest who represented their bishop and those agents who represented the count and leave the matter to them.[34]

Carloman's capitulary of Ver underscores a palpable tension in Carolingian statements about peace. On the one hand, almost all references to "peace" framed it as a relationship of harmony existing "between" parties whose very ability to enter into a peace marked them as equals—as "peers" (*pares*) in the language of the 856 capitulary of Quierzy.[35] This was true of ordinary pacts, of agreements of *fraternitas* between kings, of *convenientiae* between their leading followers, of capitulary exhortations to "peace and harmony between bishops and counts," and most notably in Alcuin's appeal for "peace and concord and unanimity between all Christian people ... whether greater or lesser." Even *coniurationes* were imagined as horizontal associations of equals. But we have also seen that the emphasis on counts and bishops being "sharers" in the royal ministry led to a growing tendency to speak of them as responsible for the "peace" of those whom they ruled on the king's behalf. In such formulations, "peace" was a state of security for the powerless. Peace meant the freedom of the powerless from violence and violation. Thus, already under Charlemagne a whole series of capitularies demanded that "churches, widows, orphans, and the less powerful shall have right peace." Those who violated "the peace of the churches of God, of widows, of orphans and wards and the less powerful" were to pay the full royal fine (*bannum*) of sixty solidi.[36] The explanation for why churches were included alongside widows and orphans as beneficiaries of "peace" is that all were among the "less powerful" who were under the protection (*mundeburdum*) of the king. But churches were themselves places of peace, and this peace was limited not just to the church itself but also to its bounded forecourt or atrium. Anyone who committed a crime or found himself liable to a vengeance killing could flee to this asylum and "have peace," be safe from harm.[37] The purpose was to establish a period of time for negotiations between the principals and their go-betweens that would allow the person taking asylum an opportunity to provide pledges and receive safe-conduct for appearing in court or going into exile.

Carolingian Peace and the Peace of God

Carolingian ideas of peace and practices of peacemaking are well worth studying in and of themselves, but the question of immediate relevance is narrower: were such ideas and practices similar or dissimilar to those of the later Peace of God? If they were similar, was this because Carolingian institutions continued to be effective in regions where the Peace of God appeared, or because those who initiated the Peace of God had access to Carolingian texts and tried to apply them, or because the societies were similar enough that similar ideas and institutions appeared in both?

Élisabeth Magnou-Nortier has presented a provocative set of answers to these questions. Two of her arguments are especially concrete and intriguing.[38] She begins by noting that sources contemporary with the early Peace councils used a distinctive lexicon to describe the kinds of violence the Peace opposed: *rapina, depraedatio, violentia, pervasio, usurpatio*. The same sources—particularly monastic sources—declaimed against a particular type of act deemed illegitimate: the imposition of "evil customs," called variously *consuetudines, exactiones, preisiones, usus, captiones, forcias, toltas*. Magnou-Nortier's first point is that the church's language of rapine was "an archaic vocabulary," which went back to the early Gallic councils of the sixth century. It was then adopted by Carolingian rulers and especially by Carolingian bishops during the reigns of Charles the Bald and his immediate successors. If this very same language was used in late tenth- and early eleventh-century sources, that does not mean that there was any great increase in violence, only that there was a renewed deployment of a traditional vocabulary in the service of ecclesiastical (especially monastic) agendas.

Magnou-Nortier's second argument is that *consuetudines*, *exactiones*, and other like terms bore a technical meaning at the time of the Peace councils and that this meaning was exactly the same as it had been in the ninth century and earlier. "Customs" and "exactions" were requisitions made by public powers for public needs. In particular, they were exactions of goods and services made to support military campaigns of the army (*exercitus*, *hostis*). Her most important evidence for the Carolingian antecedents of this aspect of the Peace of God is a collection of capitularies made by Archbishop Hincmar of Reims in the late 850s. Hincmar included eleven articles in his collection: two were from the collection of pseudo-capitularies attributed to Benedict the Deacon (Benedictus Levita); nine were from capitularies issued by Charlemagne and Louis the Pious that Hincmar took from Ansegis's important capitulary collection.[39] Comparing Hincmar's collection to key articles of the early Peace of God leaves little doubt that both were speaking of much the same thing. The first article, addressed to counts, demanded that they "show reverence to the church" and "live in concord" with bishops and aid them, "so that you may do peace and justice in your ministries" and be "aiders and defenders of orphans, widows, and the other poor and honorers of the holy church of God and its servants." Illustrating what was meant by aiding and defending the "poor," the majority of the succeeding articles concerned acts classified variously as rapine, plundering, burning, theft, forcible taking, injury, and breaking and entering (*rapere*, *praedari*, *incendere*, *furari*, *abstulere*, *dampnum facere*, *infregere*). Significantly, the prohibited actions all concerned exactions made during military campaigns, with the taking of grain and animals being singled out for particular condemnation. Magnou-Nortier correctly points out that we should not think of such actions as uncontrolled plundering and looting but as requisitions for the support of the army made beyond what was actually owed and taken from those who did not owe it. Just as significantly, the capitularies Hincmar selected categorized such actions as violations of "peace": for example, "concerning the peace to be maintained in the army's march"; "whatever misdeeds they have committed by violating peace"; "concerning peace"; "concerning peace and justice." The parallels between these articles and those of the later Peace of God are even more striking when one considers the second and the eleventh articles in Hincmar's collection. The second article insisted that the laity show reverence to bishops and priests, listen to their preaching, and observe fasts ordained by them. Above all, lay persons should keep "the Lord's day" as a holy day. To set an example for its observance, counts were prohibited from allowing judicial assemblies and markets to be held on Sundays. The eleventh article required anyone who committed any of the offences classified as "rapine" to do public or private penance, while those who committed acts of rapine against churches were to be excommunicated— "held outside the threshold of the holy mother church until they have made satisfaction to the church that they harmed." Both articles anticipate very precisely important elements of the Peace and Truce of God. For as we shall see, excommunication and penance were hallmark sanctions of the Peace, while observance of fasts and, above all, observance of Sundays were hallmark teachings of the Truce.

Such commonalities have led Magnou-Nortier and others to argue that the Peace of God was nothing new, certainly nothing revolutionary. On the contrary, it was not only well within Carolingian traditions, it simply repeated long-established rules.

Despite the importance of her insights, Magnou-Nortier probably claimed too much. First, there is a methodological problem with her argument. She and other proponents of continuity rely principally on Hincmar of Reims's writings—notably the *Collectio de raptoribus*, the above collection of capitularies on military exactions, the capitulary of Ver redacted for Carloman, and the acts of the synod of Saint-Macre. But the known manuscripts containing these works circulated almost entirely in northern France, mostly within the province of Reims itself.[40] Yet the Peace of God began in Aquitaine, and it is not clear that any copies of the above works circulated there. Admittedly, copies of Ansegis's *Collectio capitularium* did circulate in the south, including one apparently from Le Puy.[41] But Ansegis's collection comprises over 370 articles running the gamut of issues covered by Carolingian capitularies. From these, Hincmar extracted a mere handful that served his own needs. In other words, unless one had Hincmar's pronounced interest in the preservation of church property and his commitment to the idea of written law, one would be hard pressed to use Ansegis to derive the specific protections of the Peace of God.[42] Certainly the similarities between Hincmar's articles on military seizures and the rules of the Peace of God require explanation. But one must be wary of using Hincmar as evidence for Aquitainian norms a century later.

Taken to an extreme, the argument for continuity also approaches a fallacy of false equivalence: the Peace of God may have had Carolingian elements, but Carolingian peace was not the Peace of God. For if nothing else, the above discussion of Carolingian usages of "peace" has demonstrated how multifarious they were. Carolingian peace was a pact of brotherhood between kings; a cooperative relationship between counts and bishops; a state of justice and equity that these powerful ministers guaranteed in protecting the less powerful; a state of brotherhood between all Christians. West Frankish Carolingian peace was a set of agreements between a ruler's most powerful *fideles*; a set of agreements between those *fideles* and the king; an illicit *coniuratio* between individuals for self-help, mutual protection, or rebellion. To say that the Peace of God descended from Carolingian peace or simply continued it is to overlook one of the most important aspects of the Peace of God: it represented a drastic winnowing of what had been a vast, complex semiotic field.

Indeed, in its basic framing the Peace of God was entirely different from Carolingian norms. In Hincmar's collection of capitularies, as in nearly all capitularies, injunctions were usually phrased as the command or exhortation of the king or emperor. In many such capitularies, observance of the commands was enjoined on both subjects and royal ministers by virtue of their oath of fidelity to the ruler. In contrast, at least during the classic phase of the Peace and Truce of God the king had nothing to do with either the promulgation or the enforcement of their stipulations. Instead, the articles of Peace and Truce developed as the product of consensual agreements between ecclesiastical and secular elites. If they were described as a *constitutio*, its legitimacy and enforcement derived first and foremost from the oaths of those who swore to uphold what had been established. Their oaths were not made to the king nor even to the bishops or counts and apparently not even to the other swearers. In fact, the nature of its oaths is one of the strangest aspects of the Peace of God, and one of the most underinvestigated. Raoul Glaber described the

Peace as "a devout promise offered to almighty God." His statement is confirmed by the Peace of Cologne, which explicitly called its obligations "a promise made to God."[43] But Raoul also called the Peace a "pact," a detail that gives meaning to one of his most frequently quoted and misunderstood passages. For where pacts might be made with handshakes or by placing one's right hand in another's, Raoul describes the participants in the Peace assemblies raising their hands to heaven; and he calls this—what appears to be a heavenly handshake—"a sign of the perpetual pact that they promised between themselves and God."[44] This is almost unheard of. Promissory oaths could be sworn to lords or peers; they could be sworn on relics (and later gospel books) in the sight of God. One has a hard time finding oaths that were sworn *with* God to signal a pact made with Him. This is surely one reason why some critics of the Peace (notably Bishop Gerard of Cambrai) thought the Peace of God sacrilegious and guaranteed to invite perjury and therefore damnation.[45] Admittedly, Raoul's testimony that the Peace oaths established a pact with God seems unique. But then, we really do not know what the legal status of the Peace oaths was. Oddly, in some ways they most resembled the one kind of peace the Carolingians rejected: the *coniuratio*. What they were most adamantly *not* like were the vertical oaths of which the Carolingians approved.

Carolingian ideas of peace may have been necessary for the Peace of God; they were not sufficient for it.

Assembly Politics and Castles

Roger Bonnaud-Delamare argued for continuity between Carolingian ideas of peace and the Peace of God as long ago as 1939, but he did so on the basis of an untenable set of assumptions about the unchallenged importance of Augustine's notion of peace and order throughout the early Middle Ages.[46] In contrast, more recent proponents of continuity have directed their arguments against the historiographical model of a "feudal mutation."[47] This model holds that the decades around the turn of the millennium saw a complete upheaval in social and political structures, particularly in France and Catalonia. The result was a new kind of lordship over dependent peasants. Castles were its anchors. Unbridled violence accompanied its creation. The Peace of God was an attempt to control the violence. Those who deny the model often point instead to 888 as initiating a more clearly defined and obvious moment in the transformation of the West Frankish kingdom.[48] In that year, a non-Carolingian became king: Odo, margrave of Neustria. Unable to rule effectively throughout the kingdom, facing rivals who were his equals in lineage, status, and power, Odo effectively countenanced the appropriation of quasi-regalian authority by a handful of princes within the regions they controlled. At first, the major such principalities were Burgundy, Aquitaine, and Odo's own Neustria, soon joined by Flanders and Gothia and later by Normandy. Within these territories, representatives of a single family ruled as dukes or margraves. They commanded the counts who ruled under them and appointed bishops within their territories, often taking both from their own close relatives. They also commandeered the lands of churches and especially monasteries, using those lands to reward the warriors who fought for them. By the time the Carolingians were restored to the throne in 936, they had exceedingly few lands with which to recruit their own supporters or serve as the core of a royal domain that could become the territorial basis of their own principality. In these circumstances, West Frankish politics came to be even more a politics of pacts (often called *amicitiae*, "friendships"), as the great princes made (and broke) alliances not only with their peers but also with the kings themselves, who therefore no longer stood above the system of pacts but rather were part of it.[49]

However, the tenth-century "principalities" were not all that well-defined territorially. Certainly they were never territorially "bounded." They consisted of loose assemblages of counties and *pagi* which could be gained or lost by gaining or losing the allegiance of allies and clients. The principalities also never developed the kinds of political institutions that could help create a cohesive identity. In particular, they never developed a unifying princely court, in all senses of the term "court": fixed judicial courts recognized as the forum for settling disputes; regularly occurring political courts in which decisions affecting an entire principality were made by a region's elite and a prince's ministers; periodic festal courts that marked the important events of a prince's reign. This does not mean that there were no judicial assemblies. We often find them in our sources. In particular, local judicial assemblies continued to function with some regularity in the south of the kingdom (at least that is where they are most frequently attested in charters).[50] The great princes also held large assemblies in which their lay and ecclesiastical clients gathered around them; but these seem to have been summoned more or less ad hoc, as needed either for the leader's immediate political needs or to settle particularly troublesome disputes.[51] We also know that bishops continued to hold synods. Again they are especially well attested in the south of the kingdom. But here, too, it is not clear that they were held with any predictable regularity. When we see them, they seem to have been summoned to address specific problems, again usually disputes.[52]

In any case, the princes lacked the wherewithal to permanently attach subordinate families to their leadership. As a result, over time the principalities themselves fragmented into smaller lordships; or perhaps put more accurately, counts and viscounts were increasingly able to stake out positions that gave them greater freedom of political action. However, the same factors applied to counts and viscounts that had applied to dukes and margraves. They ruled the areas subject to them with the aid of close kin. They maintained their positions of power and created the means of projecting power by forging alliances with others—with peers, with lesser lords, with greater counts—as they tried to undermine the support of rivals and gain footholds in their rivals' territories. The situation has been documented in countless regions of the kingdom: in the Neustrian territories once ruled firmly by Odo and his immediate successors, where after 954 the family's former viscounts at Tours, Blois, and Anjou began executing their own policies, often against each other; in the Aquitaine of William Ironarm and William the Great, where the counts of Anjou consistently siphoned off the loyalty of the dukes' Poitevin clients; in Gothia, where the counts of Toulouse and the Rouergue steadily lost effective dominance over the viscounts of the Languedoc; in the Aquitaine of the Auvergne, where the extinction of the ducal dynasty in 927 left a welter of aristocratic kindreds without any single secular leader ruling at all.[53] As many historians have pointed out, the result was not anarchy. But military campaigns were frequent. And increasingly, castles were the centrepieces of political and military strategies.

The proliferation of castles is the one thing critics of the so-called "feudal mutation" cannot argue around. In fact, the more castles have been studied the more we have learned just how many there were. These were not the great curtained castles of the crusader states or Edward I's Welsh march. They could be wooden or stone keeps built on stone outcroppings or placed at the junction of rivers. Most often they were simple "motte and bailey" castles: an artificial mound of packed earth (the motte), averaging fifty to sixty metres in diameter; a ditch or *fosse* running around the motte; a wooden palisade encircling the plateau of the motte; the yard or "bailey" enclosed by the palisade; a wooden tower and buildings within the yard that served to house the garrison and keep stores. Admittedly, the archaeological remains of mottes can be hard to date; but there is very little doubt that they began to be built in large numbers after the middle of the tenth century and that the early eleventh century was the great age of their construction.[54] The reason is not irrelevant to the genesis of the Peace of God.

One way we know that the proliferation of castles was a new phenomenon dating to the tenth century and after was because in their heyday the Carolingians did not use castles to garrison the empire. They had no need of them. Building new, if simple, fortifications only began later in the reign of Charles the Bald in response to repeated Viking incursions along the kingdom's most vulnerable rivers. At the same time Charles established rules that determined the distribution of renders and labour services for building and maintaining castles and bridge-heads, and garrisoning and provisioning them. He specified the terms under which individuals were to serve in the army (*hostis*) and the emergency response militia (*lantweri*). He allowed counts to collect fines in lieu of service from those too poor to serve.[55] He created "marches" that kept the most threatened regions permanently mobilized. He entrusted the command of the marches to a small number of favoured aristocratic leaders. And to support their commands—in particular to allow them to recruit warriors to fight under them—he gave these leaders control of important, well-endowed monasteries and allowed them to divert the monasteries' lands to their military needs.

Because the monasteries were both centres of military command and targets of attack, they themselves were fortified with walls and towers.[56] This was why Hincmar of Reims was so concerned with "the peace of the army": the rules governing military campaigns and their provisioning were new, and newly invasive, and created new occasions for abuse, and the estates and peasants of churches were crucial to the new military commands and their support.

Castles were built not only against Vikings. They also proved their worth in the wars that began to be fought between the princes and the kings and their clients. The annals of the later ninth century show all the great monasteries and important cities and towns fortified, garrisoned on behalf of the great counts, and being the focus of their political and military strategies not just in wars against the Vikings but also in their rivalries with each other. They also mention in passing any number of unnamed castles (*castra*) as sites of sieges and objects of negotiation in the magnates' own struggles.[57] A few decades later the *Annals* of Flodoard, written contemporaneously between 922 and 966, shows counts and bishops constantly building, destroying, taking, and rebuilding castles as the primary means to hold and profit from territory. However, these castles were usually located at traditionally important political centres (the capitals of *pagi*), and Flodoard shows them being built for and controlled by the greatest leaders of the kingdom, while those who held them on their behalf were also important leaders (counts or viscounts).[58] Sources of the early eleventh century show us something quite different—a tremendous proliferation of castles built by lesser leaders whom historians usually classify broadly as "lords" or "castellans." In his *Chronicle*, for example, Ademar of Chabannes names 26 *castra*; and when he discusses the politics and warfare of the secular elite, it is invariably in terms of struggles either over such castles or fought from them.[59] From the same period and region we have an account of a series of conflicts between William the Great, duke of Aquitaine, and Hugh, lord of Lusignan. It is an immensely intriguing source because it offers a rare account of such conflicts from the point of view of the castellan. But for present purposes, the importance of the *Conventum* is that it convincingly documents the centrality of castles to the politics and warfare of Aquitaine in the 1020s. For it names thirteen different castles as the foci of claims and targets of attack by Hugh and his enemies, ten of the castles located in a narrow arc extending less than 100 kilometres south/southwest of Poitiers.[60] One might also cite the famous conventions of Catalonia and the oaths of Languedoc that fixed in precise detail the terms by which castles would be held and rendered. Hundreds of them are extant from both regions; but the series begins in the first quarter of the eleventh century.[61]

One can argue about how many of these castles were truly new in the period, though most historians have no doubt that the majority were entirely new constructions, built where there had never been castles before. But the point is not essential. What is essential is this. First, both narrative and non-narrative sources of the early eleventh century show castles as central to the creation, holding, and projection of local political power in ways that had not been true in the early tenth century, let alone the ninth. Second, the same sources show a greater number of regional political figures acting with considerable autonomy in their relations with each other and with their own nominal lords, bargaining with them, holding castles against them, and making alliances with others for their own political and military benefit. Third, the sources show that the terms on which castles were held were being spelled out in agreements of ever greater detail. Fourth, the sources documenting these trends are exactly contemporaneous with the appearance and diffusion of the Peace of God and originate precisely in the regions where the Peace of God began—in Aquitaine.

None of this necessarily means that the proliferation of castles occasioned a surge of unprecedented violence that the Peace of God was designed to remedy. The problem was not "violence" in any ordinary understanding of the word.[62] The problem was the absence of any political or jurisdictional entity that could make binding rules by either authority or consensus. This brings us to the question of why the Peace of God first appeared in Aquitaine.

Aquitaine

During the second half of the tenth century almost all West Frankish principalities lost political cohesiveness, but Aquitaine passed through a political crisis unparalleled in any other region of the kingdom. Between 893 and 918 the duke of Aquitaine was William the Pious. Although he is most famous as the founder of the monastery of Cluny in 910, Cluny and its county were actually geographically eccentric to the core of his territories. The core of his principality was the Auvergne. When William died without sons in 918, he was succeeded by his two nephews in turn. Each ruled only briefly. Each died childless. Upon the dynasty's extinction in 927 the ruling king, Raoul, refused to appoint a new duke, probably because all the likely candidates were already too powerful and because a leaderless Auvergne made Raoul's own centre of power in Burgundy more secure. Only after Raoul's death, under the newly restored Carolingian king Louis IV, do we again find a duke ruling over the Auvergne: first Raymond-Pons, count of Toulouse and margrave of Gothia, in 936, the very year of Louis's accession; then on the death of Raymond-Pons (ca. 940) his close kinsman Raymond of Rouergue, also apparently margrave of Gothia. Immediately after Louis IV's death in 954 the lords of the Auvergne went over en masse to William Towhead, count of Poitiers, and recognized him as duke.[63]

Formally, therefore, "dukes of Aquitaine" ruled the Auvergne in the middle of the tenth century. In fact, neither the margraves of Gothia nor the counts of Poitiers exercised any authority there; the region was simply too rugged and too far away, and each ruler had more pressing problems closer to home. This was the difference between the Auvergne and all the other regions of the kingdom: the absence of any single secular prince who could act as leader, whose rule could provide a focus for political manoeuvring, whose assemblies could provide an occasion for periodic political reunions of a region's elite. It is not that the Auvergne disintegrated into anarchy (though there are signs of power struggles backed up by military actions), but in staving off anarchy and regulating conflicts, the Auvergnat nobility came to conduct its politics quite differently from other regions. Far more than anywhere else in the kingdom, its elites created alliances with each other and acted collectively. They intermarried in ways that created a bewildering number of cross-cutting kinship ties. They founded or reformed monasteries and used the monasteries to give a spiritual dimension to their alliances. Significantly, the key figures in these alliance networks were bishops: first Godescalc, bishop of Le Puy, then Stephen II, bishop of Clermont. Both came from the region's leading families and were related to all its other leading families. They were the ones who sponsored the monastic foundations and reforms that sealed the alliances between families. They were the crucial figures who represented the Auvergne when Aquitainians had to deal with outside rulers, including the kings. And they held assemblies. In 955, when William Towhead of Poitiers received the homage of the "lords of the Auvergne" (*seniores Arvernici*), it was done in an assembly at Ennezat (site of the major assemblies of the old dukes of Aquitaine) apparently summoned by Bishop Stephen, who also seems to have been the principal negotiator between William, the magnates, and the king.[64] Three years later Stephen organized an assembly at Clermont attended by "lay lords, clerics, and monks," its purpose to end a period of warfare among the "princes of the Auvergne" (*principes Arvernorum*).[65] In 972 Stephen used the dedication of the new church of Aurillac to sponsor another assembly. This one was attended by the bishops of Périgord and Cahors and "all the clergy and a countless multitude of people," while its decrees were made "by the counsel of the clergy of the see of Auvergne and other noble men." If we can trust the charter that records the event, the purpose was to establish Aurillac as the site of regular judicial assemblies governing a fixed territory surrounding Aurillac.[66]

What we see in the Auvergne to a much greater degree than anywhere else in the kingdom is the use of assemblies at which lay aristocrats gathered together under the leadership of bishops who held everything together in the absence of a prince.

This unique situation formed the background of the first event that looks something like a Peace assembly: a meeting near Le Puy in or soon after 975. The initiator of the meeting was the new bishop of Le Puy, Wido. His brother was Geoffrey Greymantle, count of Anjou. His sister was Adelaide, widow of one of the most powerful Auvergnat lords. Adelaide's sons were counts of the Gévaudan and controlled Saint-Julien of Brioude, the most important secular monastery of the Auvergne. Wido had been "parachuted" into the Auvergne as bishop in 975 as part of a plan by Wido's brother and the king to control the region. Yet as an outsider, he did not enjoy the kind of mul-

tiplex, cross-generational alliances that had made Godescalc of Le Puy and Stephen of Clermont so powerful. He
had to use more force to assert his position. Luckily he had
it, since his nephews were nearby counts, and the bishops
of Le Puy were themselves ex officio counts of the Velay.
But he had to move quickly. So probably shortly after his
arrival, "he ordered all the knights and peasants of his diocese to gather as one so that he might hear their counsel
about bringing peace to reign." The meeting occurred at
Saint-Germain-Laprade, in open fields located about six
miles east of his city. When everyone had gathered, Wido
"asked that they swear a peace, that they not oppress
the properties of the poor and churches, and that they
restore what they had [unjustly] taken, so that they might
conduct themselves like faithful Christians as was proper."
The assembly refused his request. Anticipating the rejec-
tion, before the meeting Wido had ordered his nephews to
bring their armies (*exercitus*) to Brioude. After the assembly refused to take the oath, Wido had his nephews move
their armies during the night. They were at Laprade by
the morning. Surrounded, the members of the assembly
had no choice. Everyone swore the oath, gave hostages to
ensure that they kept the peace, and restored the lands
and castles (*castella*) of the cathedral and the goods of
churches they had seized (*rapuerunt*).[67]

Our only source for these events is a kind of episcopal
gesta written down in the twelfth century, so one must be
careful not to push its account too hard. Still, the author
appears to have used earlier records, for his language is
that of the late tenth and early eleventh centuries. In any
case, the event is too important to ignore. What happened
at Laprade was not quite the Peace of God. The forum for
the oaths was not an assembly uniting bishops of several
dioceses. It involved the bishop of just one diocese, and
even he acted as count as much as bishop. The oaths were

coerced by the threat of imminent armed force, which is not mentioned for other Peace councils. Conversely, the characteristic sanction of the Peace—excommunication— was apparently not even considered at Laprade. There is no mention of the crowds of commoners frequently attested in Peace councils, nor of monks and relics and miracles. Finally, there is no hint of the specific articles that came to define the Peace of God, articles that specifically protected the unarmed and their properties from attacks. What Laprade does show is this: by the 970s, in a region whose most distinctive trait was the absence of any unitary secular political authority, a bishop was cooperating with counts to hold assemblies at which collective oaths were seen as crucial to an effort "to make peace reign." And the most important element of this peace was an agreement not to plunder the properties of churches and the poor.

Notes

[1] For the meaning of peace in the Roman Empire, see Greg Woolf, "Roman Peace," in *War and Society in the Roman World*, ed. J. Rich and G. Shipley (New York: Routledge, 1993), pp. 171–94; Jean-François Thomas, "De la paix des armes à la tranquillité de l'âme: étude lexicale de *pax* et de certains 'synonymes,'" *Revue des études latines* 89 (2011): 56–75.

[2] R. A. Markus, *Saeculum: History and Society in the Theology of St. Augustine* (Cambridge: Cambridge University Press, 1970).

[3] *City of God*, 19.13, trans. Henry Paolucci, *The Political Writings of St. Augustine* (Washington, DC: Regnery, 1996), pp. 143–44.

[4] Paul J. E. Kershaw, *Peaceful Kings: Peace, Power, and the Early Medieval Imagination* (Oxford: Oxford University Press, 2011), pp. 64–68.

[5] *Lex Romana Visigothorum*, ed. G. F. Haenel (Berlin, 1849), 1.1, pp. 338–40.

[6] For example, MGH Formulae, *Formulae Andecavenses*, nos. 26, 45, 55; *Formulae Turonenses*, no. 25; *Marculfi Formulae*, 2.13, 14, 18.

[7] MGH Formulae, *Marculfi Formulae*, 2.14, 18.

[8] Alexander Callander Murray, "From Roman to Frankish Gaul: 'Centenarii' and 'Centenae' in the Administration of the Merovingian Kingdom," *Traditio* 44 (1988): 59–100 at 80–84.

[9] Jégou, *L'évêque, juge de paix.*

[10] *Concilia Gallia, A. 314–A. 506*, ed. C. Munier, Corpus Christianorum Series Latina 148 (Turnhout: Brepols, 1963), pp. 57–58, 177–78 (c. 2), 238–39.

[11] *Concilia Gallia, A. 511–A. 695*, ed. C. de Clercq, Corpus Christianorum Series Latina 148A (Turnhout: Brepols, 1963), p. 284 (c. 11), 274–86, 290–97.

[12] Jennifer Davis, *Charlemagne's Practice of Empire* (Cambridge: Cambridge University Press, 2015).

[13] *Die Admonitio generalis Karls des Großen*, ed. Hubert Mordek et al., MGH Fontes Iuris Germanici Antiqui in usum scholarum separatim editi 16 (Hanover: Hahnsche Buchhandlung, 2012), cc. 60–61, p. 310, with pp. 47–63.

[14] For example, MGH Capit. 1, no. 121, pp. 238–40 (801–12).

[15] MGH Conc. 1, pp. 251–52, c. 12 (Arles), 261, c. 5 (Mainz), 277, c. 20 (Chalon), 290, c. 32 (Tours); Kershaw, *Peaceful Kings* (above, n. 4).

[16] MGH Capit. 1, p. 303, c. 2.

[17] MGH Capit. 1, no. 136, p. 270; MGH Capit. 2, no. 197, c. 1, p. 54.

[18] MGH Capit. 2, no. 205 (Meersen II), c. 6, p. 73, *Adnuntiatio Karoli*, p. 74.

[19] MGH Capit. 2, no. 276, c. 2.

[20] Mayke De Jong, *The Penitential State: Authority and Atonement in the Age of Louis the Pious, 814–840* (Cambridge: Cambridge University Press, 2009).

[21] MGH Capit. 1, no. 150, c. 7, p. 304.

[22] MGH Conc. 3, no. 14, c. 4, p. 165; MGH Conc. 1, no. 36, c. 5, p. 261.

[23] MGH Capit. 1, no. 45, c. 6, p. 128.

[24] MGH Capit. 1, no. 136, p. 271, prologue and c. 4.

[25] Nithard, *Histoire des fils de Louis le Pieux*, ed. Philippe Lauer (Paris: H. Champion, 1926), 3.5–6.

[26] MGH Capit. 2, no. 204, pp. 68–71; Reinhard Schneider, *Brüdergemeinde und Schwurfreundschaft: Der Auflösungsprozeß des Karlingerreiches im Spiegel der Caritas-Terminologie in den Verträgen der karlingischen Teilkönige des 9. Jahrhunderts* (Lübeck: Matthiesen, 1964).

[27] MGH Capit. 2, no. 254, pp. 253–55. Among the many works on Coulaines, see especially Adelheid Krah, *Die Entstehung der 'potestas regia' im Westfrankenreich während der ersten Regierungsjahre Kaiser Karls II. (840–877)* (Berlin: Akademie Verlag, 2000), pp. 205–49; Kosto, "*Convenientia*," pp. 18–21.

[28] Otto Gerhard Oexle, "Conjuratio und Gilde im frühen Mittelalter: Ein Beitrag zum Problem der sozialgeschichtlichen Kontinuität zwischen Antike und Mittelalter," in *Gilden und Zünfte: Kaufmännische und gewerbliche Genossenschaften im frühen und hohen Mittelalter*, ed. Berent Schwineköper, Vorträge und Forschungen 29 (Sigmaringen: J. Thorbecke, 1985), pp. 151–214.

[29] MGH Capit. 1, no. 44, c. 10, p. 124.

[30] MGH Conc. 3, no. 14, c. 5, p. 165.

[31] MGH Conc. 3, no. 47, p. 482, ll. 3–7.

[32] MGH Capit. 1, no. 44, c. 9, p. 124; Philippe Depreux, "Les Carolingiens et le serment," in *Oralité et lien social au Moyen Âge (Occident, Byzance, Islam): Parole donnée, foi jurée, serment*, ed. Marie-France Auzépy and Guillaume Saint-Guillain (Paris: Association des amis du Centre d'histoire et civilisation de Byzance, 2009), pp. 63–80.

[33] MGH Capit. 1, no. 20, c. 16, p. 51, no. 148, c. 7, p. 301; Oexle, "Conjuratio und Gilde," pp. 152–53 (above, n. 28).

[34] MGH Capit. 2, no. 287, c. 14, p. 375: "Ne collectam faciant, quam vulgo geldam vocant, contra illos, qui aliquid rapuerint."

[35] MGH Capit. 2, no. 262, c. 10, p. 281.

[36] MGH Capit. 1, no. 68, c. 1, p. 157, no. 98, c. 2, p. 205; Bonnaud-Delamare, *L'idée de paix*, pp. 178–79.

[37] MGH Capit. 1, no. 39, c. 3, p. 113: "in atrio ipsius ecclesiae pacem habeat ..."

[38] Magnou-Nortier, "Les évêques et la paix"; Magnou-Nortier, "La place du Concile du Puy"; Magnou-Nortier, "Les mauvaises coutumes"; Magnou-Nortier, "The Enemies of the Peace."

[39] MGH Conc. 3, no. 38 (Quierzy, 857), pp. 383–98 at 394–96, with the *Collectio de raptoribus*, pp. 392–94.

[40] Hubert Mordek, *Bibliotheca capitularium regum Francorum manuscripta: Überlieferung und Traditionszusammenhang der fränkischen Herrschererlasse*, MGH Hilfsmittel 15 (Munich: MGH, 1995), pp. 386–87, 454, 488, 499–500, 507, 513, 574, 587–88, 600–3, 730–31, 780, 1029–39; Wilfried Hartmann, "Unbekannte Kanones aus dem Westfrankenreich des 10. Jahrhunderts," *Deutsches Archiv für Erforschung des Mittelalters* 43 (1987): 28–45 at 28–29.

[41] *Die Kapitulariensammlung des Ansegis*, ed. Gerhard Schmitz, MGH Capitularia regum Francorum, nova series 1 (Hanover: Hahnsche Buchhandlung, 1996), pp. 115–17, 130–32, 189–90.

[42] *Hincmar of Rheims: Life and Work*, ed. Rachel Stone and Charles West (Manchester: Manchester University Press, 2015), especially Simon Corcoran, "Hincmar and his Roman Legal Sources," pp. 129–55, and Philippe Depreux, "*Hincmar et la loi* Revisited: On Hincmar's Use of Capitularies," pp. 156–69.

[43] MGH Const. 1, no. 424, cc. 13–14, p. 605; Goetz, "Der Kölner Gottesfriede," pp. 66–68.

[44] Rodulfus Glaber, 4.16, pp. 196–97: "que deuota sponsione omnipotenti Domino offerre decreuerant"; "signum perpetui pacti de hoc quod spoponderant inter se et Deum."

[45] Barthélemy, *L'An mil*, pp. 449–54, 464; Riches, "The Peace of God"; Sam Janssens, "Context or Text? Towards a New Interpretation of Gerard I of Cambrai's Oration on the Three Orders," *The Medieval Low Countries* 3 (2016): 21–37.

[46] Bonnaud-Delamare, *L'idée de paix*.

[47] For a good introduction to a vast bibliography, see Charles West, *Reframing the Feudal Revolution: Political and Social Transformation Between Marne and Moselle, c. 800–c. 1100* (Cambridge: Cambridge University Press, 2013).

[48] Dominique Barthélemy, *L'ordre seigneurial: XIe–XIIe siècle* (Paris: Seuil, 1990).

[49] Geoffrey Koziol, *The Politics of Memory and Identity in Car-*

olingian Royal Diplomas: The West Frankish Kingdom (840–987) (Turnhout: Brepols, 2012), chaps. 5–6; Jean Dunbabin, *France in the Making, 843–1180*, 2nd ed. (Oxford: Oxford University Press, 2000), chap. 4.

[50] Jeffrey Bowman, *Shifting Landmarks: Property, Proof, and Dispute in Catalonia around the Year 1000* (Ithaca: Cornell University Press, 2004).

[51] Guillot, "Formes, fondements," pp. 85–86, 94.

[52] Isolde Schröder, *Die westfränkischen Synoden von 888 bis 987 und ihre Überlieferung*, MGH Hilfsmittel 3 (Munich: MGH, 1980), for example, nos. 30–32, 34, 39, 41, 43, 46–50, 52–53, 56–59, 62–65, 67, 70, 74.

[53] Guillot, "Formes, fondements"; Dunbabin, *France in the Making*, chap. 4 (above, n. 49); Christian Lauranson-Rosaz, *L'Auvergne et ses marges (Velay, Gévaudan) du VIIIe au XIe siècle: la fin du monde antique?* (Le Puy-en-Velay: Cahiers de la Haute-Loire, 1987); Débax, *La Féodalité languedocienne*, chap. 1. Also K.-F. Werner, "L'acquisition par la maison de Blois des comtés de Chartres et de Châteaudun," in *Mélanges de numismatique, d'archéolgie et d'histoire offerts à Jean Lafaurie* (Paris: Société de numismatique, 1980), pp. 265–72; Yves Sassier, "Thibaud le Tricheur et Hugues le Grand," in *Pays de Loire et Aquitaine de Robert le Fort aux premiers Capétiens*, ed. O. Guillot and R. Favreau (Poitiers: Société des Antiquaires de l'Ouest et des Musées de Poitiers, 1997), pp. 145–57 at 154; Bernard S. Bachrach, "Geoffrey Greymantle, Count of the Angevins, 960–987: A Study in French Politics," *Studies in Medieval and Renaissance History* 17 (1985): 1–67; Bachrach, *Fulk Nerra, the Neo-Roman Consul, 987–1040* (Berkeley: University of California Press, 1993).

[54] See especially Luc Bourgeois, "*Castrum* et habitat des élites: France et ses abords (vers 880–vers 1000)," in *Cluny: Les moines et la société au premier âge féodal*, ed. Dominique Iogna-Prat et al. (Rennes: Presses universitaires de Rennes, 2013), pp. 471–94. Also Michel Bur, *Le château*, Typologie des sources du moyen âge occidental 79 (Turnhout: Brepols, 1999); *Sites défensifs et sites fortifiés au Moyen Âge entre Loire et Pyrénées: Actes du premier colloque Aquitania, Limoges, 20–22 mai 1987*, Aqvitania, supplément 4 (1990), especially the articles by Bernadette Barrière, Geneviève Cantié, and André Debord.

[55] Simon Coupland, "The Fortified Bridges of Charles the Bald," *Journal of Medieval History* 17 (1991): 1–12; Coupland, "The Carolingian Army and the Struggle against the Vikings," *Viator* 35 (2004):

49–70. Since Coupland minimizes the significance of broad references in annals to *castella*, still valuable is Fernand Vercauteren, "Comment s'est-on défendu au IXᵉ siècle dans l'empire franc contre les invasions normandes?," *Annales du XXXᵉ congrès de la Fédération archéologique et historique de Belgique* 30 (1935–36): 117–32.

[56] Koziol, *The Politics of Memory*, chap. 4 (above, n. 49).

[57] *Annales Vedastini*, ed. B. von Simson, MGH SRG 12 (Hanover: Hahn, 1909), pp. 70–73, 76–81; *The Annals of St-Bertin*, trans. Janet L. Nelson (Manchester: Manchester University Press, 1991), pp. 171–72 (a. 871), 183 (a. 873), 206–07 (a. 878), 221 (a. 880), 222 (a. 881), 224–26 (a. 882). This is consistent with recent archaeological findings: Bourgeois, *"Castrum"* (above, n. 54).

[58] For example, Mézières, Omont, Épernay, Chièvremont, Saint-Quentin, Château-Thierry, Mont-Saint-Jean, Eu, Coucy, Durfos, Vitry, and Montreuil: *Les Annales de Flodoard*, ed. Philippe Lauer (Paris: Picard, 1906), pp. 2–3 (a. 920), 8–9, 11 (a. 922), 15 (a. 923), 25 (a. 924), 31 (a. 925), 39 (a. 927), 42 (a. 928), 44 (a. 929), etc. Flodoard also indicates that during active campaigns the great princes "laid out castles" ("castra metatus est"), but these seem to be simple, temporary earthworks long used for specific campaigns.

[59] Bernard S. Bachrach, "Early Medieval Fortifications in the 'West' of France: A Revised Technical Vocabulary," *Technology and Culture* 16 (1975): 531–69 at 549.

[60] George Beech et al., *Le Conventum (vers 1030): Un précurseur aquitain des premières épopées* (Geneva: Librairie Droz, 1995), pp. 123–58. On this vexed text, see Dominique Barthélemy, "Du nouveau sur le *Conventum Hugonis*?," *Bibliothèque de l'École des Chartes* 153 (1995): 483–95, with references.

[61] Débax, *La Féodalité languedocienne*, chap. 2; Kosto, *"Convenientia"*; Kosto, *Making Agreements in Medieval Catalonia: Power, Order, and the Written Word, 1000–1200* (Cambridge: Cambridge University Press, 2001).

[62] Warren Brown, *Violence in Medieval Europe* (New York: Longman, 2011).

[63] Lauranson-Rosaz, *L'Auvergne*, pp. 78–83 (above, n. 53); Koziol, *The Politics of Memory*, pp. 283–87, 294–303 (above, n. 49).

[64] *Cluny* I, no. 825.

[65] CJS, no. *3693*.

[66] Christian Lauranson-Rosaz, "La 'charte de Landeyrat,'" in *Autour de Gerbert d'Aurillac, le pape de l'an mil*, ed. Olivier Guyotjeannin and Emmanuel Poulle (Paris: École des Chartes, 1996), pp. 8–11.

[67] "Chronicon monasterii sancti Petri Aniciensis," in *Cartulaire de l'abbaye de Saint-Chaffre du Monastier*, ed. Ulysse Chevalier (Paris, 1884), pp. 151–66 at 152; Lauranson-Rosaz, *L'Auvergne*, pp. 414–16 (above, n. 53); Bernard S. Bachrach, "The Northern Origins of the Peace Movement at Le Puy in 975," *Historical Reflections / Réflexions Historiques* 14 (1987): 405–21.

Chapter 2

The Peace of God

The Peace of God appeared at the very moment when our sources increase markedly in both variety and number, so we are not poorly informed about the movement: we have conciliar decrees, chronicle accounts, hagiographical narratives, charters, and letters. Why, then, has the Peace of God been so difficult for historians to grasp? The most important reason is that different types of sources give us significantly different representations of the movement. And somewhat paradoxically, the fullest, most circumstantial accounts are among the most problematic, even though they are the ones most frequently relied upon by historians to describe the movement and its purposes.

Take, for example, the most famous of these accounts, that offered by Raoul Glaber in his *Histories*. He describes a series of troubling events at the approach of the millennium of Christ's Passion (that is, 1033): first the deaths of many important men, then three years of heavy rains that made it difficult to plant crops, and a famine so severe that people turned to cannibalism. It seemed clear that "the order of the seasons and the elements ... had fallen into perpetual chaos, and with it had come the end of mankind." But when the millennium of the Passion arrived, the weather cleared and the famine ended. And now Peace councils were summoned, first in Aquitaine, then in Provence, then in Burgundy, eventually reaching "the furthest corners of the French realm." Everyone attended the councils when summoned, "great, middling, and poor ... rejoicing and ready, one and all, to obey the commands of the clergy no less than if they had been given by a voice from heaven speaking to men on earth." At these councils lists of prohibited actions were drawn up and oaths were sworn "for keeping an inviolable peace." All men, no matter what their status, were free to go about without fear of armed attack. Seizure of the property of others was to be sanctioned by fines and harsh corporal punishment. Churches were to be held in honour, and the asylum offered by churches to fleeing criminals was to be respected, save for someone "who violated the pact of the peace." Clerics, monks, and nuns were to be free from attack while travelling, as were those travelling with them. At these gatherings the sick were healed, the limbs of the lame and crippled were straightened.

> And all cried out with one voice to God, their hands extended: "Peace! Peace! Peace!" This was the sign of their perpetual covenant with God.[68]

How could any historian resist such a story, particularly as it provides sense and context for the often fragmentary, contextless decrees of the councils themselves? In Raoul's account, the Peace of God was a millenarian movement. It peaked at the millennium of Christ's Passion following a period of famine and disease viewed as God's punishment for sin. It was a mass movement, gathering not just elites but also commoners. Its purpose was to establish a kind of peace on earth of the sort first announced by angels at the birth of Christ.[69]

Unfortunately, Raoul Glaber is not the most trustworthy of historians. But then few writers of history during the period are trustworthy, least of all those like Raoul who

were most proud of their learning. For what their educa-
tion taught them was that historians were not supposed to
adhere to facts. They were supposed to explain the meaning of facts and elicit a moral lesson from them, even if
that meant distorting dates and events.[70] So throughout
his *Histories* Raoul groups together events of widely dispa-
rate dates to suggest some convergence of eschatological
signs. He repeatedly introduces millenarian expectations
at this or that moment to demonstrate the imminence of
God's judgement, then drops them, then reintroduces them
again, all to illustrate Christian history's recurring pattern:
God threatens; mankind repents; God forgives; mankind
backslides. Furthermore, his account of the Peace cannot
be made to conform to the sequence of known councils.
As Dominique Barthélemy has remarked, it seems obvious
that Raoul was describing an ideal type of a Peace council.[71] As for his association of the Peace assemblies with
millennial hopes, it is unclear how far we can rely on his
testimony; for Raoul was a monk, raised at Saint-Germain
of Auxerre, professed at Saint-Bénigne of Dijon, later res-
ident at Cluny. And all three monasteries were centres of
intense interest in eschatology. Admittedly, their interest
did not lie in dating the coming millennium. Rather, they
foregrounded the Last Judgement as the moment when
the damned and saved would be separated for eternity.
The purity of the lives of monks, their intercessory prayers
and masses for their lay patrons' salvation, the donation of
properties to monasteries by the laity in return for prayers
and masses: all this was justified by the inevitability of
a Final Judgement.[72] Another important chronicler of the
Peace of God was Ademar of Chabannes. His writings are
also peppered with apocalyptic warnings, and he, too, was
a monk, of Saint-Cybard of Angoulême.[73] As evidence of
a millenarian spirit that fed the Peace of God, historians
have frequently cited the eschatological warnings found

in the prologues of charters, especially charters written by monks to record donations made to monasteries by laymen and laywomen.[74] In other words, it is monastic sources and almost exclusively monastic sources that provide a sense of the eschatological backdrop of the Peace of God. The conciliar decrees themselves, largely the work of bishops and the product of negotiations between them and powerful lay lords, provide no evidence for any eschatological concerns whatsoever.

The Peace councils have also been seen as the moment when "the common people" became a political force, as monks and bishops used the opportunity of the Peace councils to mobilize the latent power of popular opinion.[75] But here, too, we must be cautious; for evidence of the participation of "the masses" is also especially pronounced in narratives written by monks like Raoul, Ademar, Andrew of Fleury, and the often anonymous authors who described the miracles that supposedly accompanied the assemblies. For dwelling on the size of crowds and their social diversity had been a conceit of writings about relic translations going back to Vitricius of Rouen. Since by the eleventh century monks had become the saints' preferred intercessors for humanity and guardians of the saints' relics, such emphases became particularly pronounced in monastic writings about relics and their translations and miracles.

Yet scepticism can be taken too far. Although earlier monastic writers had been deeply invested in eschatology, Raoul Glaber and Ademar of Chabannes were truly unusual in the doggedness with which they sought out specific contemporary signs of a coming millennium. More important, the heyday of the Peace of God was bookended by two explicit attestations of contemporary belief in the imminence of the End Time. First, writing towards the end of the tenth century Abbo of Fleury recalled that in his youth he had heard a preacher in Paris declare that after 1,000 years Antichrist would appear, the Last Judgement coming soon after. He added that his own late abbot Richard (963–78) had received letters from Lotharingia reporting a rumour that had spread "nearly throughout the whole world," according to which "without doubt" the world would end when the feast of the Annunciation occurred on Good Friday.[76] The significance of the conjunction was that the Annunciation, celebrating Christ's Incarnation, was observed on March 25, thought to have been the historical date of Christ's death on the Cross on Good Friday. That is, Christ's Second Coming would occur on the same date as his First. The identical belief appears in the second event. In late 1064 pilgrims set out from Germany for the Holy Sepulchre in Jerusalem, 7,000 strong and more, led by some of the greatest and most learned prelates in Germany but also including secular princes and masses of the humble. At least some of the pilgrims were motivated by the belief that the next Easter would occur on the very date of Christ's historical Resurrection and inaugurate the Last Judgement.[77] In between these events, when the first stage of the Peace movement was at its height, a monk of Saint-Vaast of Arras made a marginal notation in a computistic table under the year 1000. Calling attention to a large earthquake that had occurred that year, he wrote: "These and other signs predicted having been completed by divine operation, our hope is made more certain in the sight of all regarding those that remain to be completed in due order."[78] A few decades later, a source critical of the Peace propagated at Amiens and Corbie in the 1030s made fun of those who promoted it by brandishing what they claimed was a letter fallen from heaven.[79] Such letters are well known. Two of them are now in the Bibliothèque nationale in Paris, having fallen there not from heaven but from Corbie itself. The letters demand that all Christians keep the Lord's Day and the saints' feast days, that they pray, fast, and attend church, that they avoid false oaths and do penance for their sins. If they do not heed these warnings the Lord will send hail, storms, and famine, and destroy them as he destroyed Sodom and Gomorrah. He has already sent two letters, the letter concludes. This is the third. There will be no more warnings.[80] Though these exemplars were copied at Corbie in the twelfth century, their concerns show unmistakable overlap with the themes of the Truce of God as it was preached in the eleventh century, particularly the need for fasting, the observance of Sunday, the horror of perjury, the veneration of saints' days, and the need for penance.[81] Admittedly, the letters are not millenarian. Strictly speaking, they are not even Apocalyptic, for it is not necessarily the Last Judgement that is imminent but only a divine judgement. Nevertheless, their threat of judgement, damnation, and punishment certainly makes them "apocalyptic" in a broader sense. But once more, it is a source from a monastery that tells us of these aspects of the Peace of Amiens and Corbie, not any statutes of Peace.[82]

Similarly, the participation of the "masses" in Peace assemblies may not merely be a hagiographical topos beloved by monks. It could be an aspect of the Peace of God that monastic sources reveal and the statutes occlude. For example, the *Liber miraculorum sancte Fidis* tells an interesting story about a Peace assembly held by the bishop of Rodez and the countess of Rouergue in the early eleventh century. The author names four saints whose relics were brought and mentions an image of Mary as well. All were set out in pavilions in a field about a mile from the city. Miracles were worked, including one by St. Faith, who cured a boy in such spectacular fashion that a great roar went up from the crowd of "commoners." Hearing the racket, the bishop, the countess, and the other "lords of the council," who were holding their deliberations some distance away (*remotiores*), asked each other, "What is all this clamor from the people about (*ista popularis conclamatio*)?" They did not know because they and the people were at entirely different locations. The "commoners" (*vulgi*) were with the saints in the field; the "lords of the council" (*seniores concilii*) were with each other.[83]

We must therefore be careful when discussing millenarian and popular fervour in the Peace movement. It was present. But it was not omnipresent. As at Rodez, the *seniores* and the *vulgi* may not have inhabited the same space or experienced quite the same events. The decrees of the Peace councils are themselves the best evidence of this, for they offer scarcely a hint of millenarian expectations and popular pressures that feature in so many monastic accounts. On the contrary, as we will see, one of the most important attributes of the conciliar decrees is that they are pragmatic, hard-headed, worldly, and aristocratic. Before we can understand the importance of these traits, we should gain something of an overview of the movement.

The Peace Councils

The first surviving statement of the propositions that came to be known as the "Peace of God" was issued at the Council of Charroux, held in 989. Earlier events like the assembly at Le Puy around 975 may have presaged the Peace, perhaps even already "invented" it, but the sources for them are neither contemporary enough nor detailed enough to allow certainty. Nevertheless, there is good reason to believe that Charroux really was the first true Peace council. For one thing, its bishops stated that councils had not been held for a very long time, which suggests that they thought they were doing something new. Their assembly also bore all the hallmarks one associates with Peace assemblies in ways that the possible antecedents do not. It brought together bishops of different dioceses and even provinces. The context for their gathering was relentless famine, explained as a sign of God's anger for sinfulness, the bishops implying that their decrees were a way to appease his anger. Monasteries and their relics featured prominently in the penumbra of the meeting, and the relics' public display fostered miracles. One of the primary purposes of the relics was for the swearing of oaths by which those in attendance agreed to uphold the council's stipulations—and if any single attribute defined Peace councils, it was just such oaths. Finally, we have at least four decrees of the council (originally there may well have been more, the manuscript tradition being fragmentary). Three of the four formed the core of every subsequent declaration of the Peace of God. Indeed, a few years later the Peace of Poitiers explicitly referred to the canons of Charroux as the basis for its own decrees.[84] Because they are short and so important, one might quote them in full in order to provide some sense for the kind of stipulations we are dealing with.

1. If anyone breaks into a holy church or takes anything from it by force, unless he hasten to make satisfaction let him be anathema.

2. If anyone plunders sheep, oxen, asses, cows, or male and female goats of peasants (*agricolarum*) and other poor persons, unless it be for their own fault, if he fails to make reparation for everything, let him be anathema.

3. If anyone attacks or seizes or strikes a priest or deacon or any person of the clergy who is not bearing arms (that is, shield, sword, breastplate, or helmet) but is simply walking about or staying in a house—unless he [the victim] has been found guilty of some

fault after examination by his own bishop—he [the attacker] shall be regarded as sacrilegious, and unless he makes satisfaction he shall be kept outside the threshold of the holy church of God.[85]

Over the next eleven years there were at least four Peace councils and perhaps as many as seven: Narbonne (ca. 990, poorly attested); Limoges (994); Anse (994); Saint-Paulien outside Le Puy (993 or 994); Lalbenque near Cahors (after 994, very poorly attested); Rodez (ca. 1000); and Poitiers (probably 999/1000). All these councils occurred south of the Loire; all but Anse occurred in what one might call "Greater Aquitaine."[86] The presence of monks and their relics and the working of miracles featured ever more prominently in these gatherings. But the councils also expanded and honed the decisions taken at Charroux. This was especially visible at Saint-Paulien, whose decrees survive in a fairly complete form, sometimes close to the words actually sworn.[87] In paraphrase:

- No one shall enter a church by force.

- No one shall take as plunder (*predam*) horses, cattle, asses, or the loads they bear, nor sheep, goats, or pigs, nor shall they kill them.

- Clerics shall not carry arms.

- No one shall injure monks or those travelling with them who are not bearing arms.

- No one shall hold a serf (*villanum, villanam*) for ransom (*redemptionem*).

- No one shall exact any "evil custom" (*mala consuetudine*) from lands of churches, bishops, chapters, and monasteries.

- No one shall seize traders or merchants (*negociatores*).

- No layman shall hold church offerings or burial fees.

- All who violate these rules shall be excommunicated until they make satisfaction.

After 1015 the Peace of God entered Burgundy in a series of councils, the best known being those of Verdun-sur-le-Doubs (1021–22?) and Héry (1024), though councils were also held at Dijon, Beaune, Lyon, and Vienne.[88] The oath associated with Verdun was one of the most elaborate and specific yet formulated. In 1023, Bishops Warin of Beauvais and Berold of Soissons submitted a version of it to the king of France for his approval. The occasion was a major assembly held at the royal palace of Compiègne attended by some of the most important princes of the realm, notably the count of Flanders and the duke of Normandy.[89] In 1033/34 an apparently much more radical Peace was sworn at Amiens and Corbie, and perhaps also at Oudenaarde in Flanders around 1030.[90] But there may have been strong reactions against its terms, so the Peace of God in northern France tended to develop from the 1023 Peace of Compiègne. At various dates that are hard to pin down, some version of it was sworn at Laon and Cambrai (1034–35?),[91] at Thérouanne (1042/43 and ca. 1060),[92] at Soissons (1092/93), and at Saint-Omer (1099).[93] Some of its elements were authorized by Pope Leo IX at the Council of Reims in 1049.[94] The Peace also appeared in Normandy: at Caen in 1042/43 and again in 1061/62; at Lisieux in 1064; at Lillebonne in 1080; at Rouen in 1096. Meanwhile, the Peace had continued to develop in the south of France. There were declarations of the Peace at Poitiers (ca. 1010, ca. 1030), Anse (1025), Toulouges (1027 and ca. 1041), Charroux (1027/28), probably Bourges and Limoges (1031), Vic (1030, 1033), Le Puy (after 1031), Mende (before 1036), Périgueux (1037/59), Arles (1037/41), Saint-Gilles (1041/42), Albi (1041/42), Narbonne (before

1041/42 and in 1054), and so on. At a certain point, one simply loses track.[95]

During this succession of councils the stipulations of the Peace grew more and more specific. One set of stipulations became particularly important. Known as the Truce of God (*Treuga Dei*), it first appeared in 1027 at the above-mentioned council at Toulouges (in the shadow of the Pyrenees near Perpignan). "In honor of the Lord's day," it prohibited all acts of violence of any sort between Saturday afternoon and Monday morning. In 1030, a council at Vic extended the days of the Truce from Thursday evening to Monday morning.[96] In 1033, again at Vic, another council not only retained the exemption of these days from any hostile actions but added the three major periods of the liturgical calendar and a large number of feast days: from Advent to the octave of Epiphany; from the beginning of Lent to the octave of Easter; from the beginning of the Rogation Days to the octave of Pentcost; the four Ember Days; the feasts of the Apostles, Mary, All Saints, and St. Peter in Chains; the feasts of the Discovery of the Cross and the Veneration of the Cross; the feast days commemorating the dedication of the cathedral churches of the subscribing bishops; the feast days of the chief patron saints of those churches; and the vigils of all these days.[97] The Truce of God continued to spread along these lines throughout the Mediterranean regions of the kingdom until by the time of the Council of Narbonne in 1054, the Truce not only covered most of these same days and periods (with the substitution of the feast days of locally important saints) but also ran every ordinary week from Wednesday at sundown to Monday at sunrise.[98] It has been estimated that at its most expansive, only eighty days a year were left uncovered by the Truce of God.[99] After 1041 this Truce was also adopted throughout much of the north of the kingdom, albeit apparently without the inclusion of so many feast days, so that most of the instances of the Peace of God from northern France mentioned above also included the some version Truce of God.[100]

However, this brief account glosses over many problems. One example concerns the Peace assemblies of Limoges and Bourges. Everyone is agreed that an important assembly was held at Limoges in 994; but was an even larger assembly held there in 1031? Historians long thought so, because the deliberations at Limoges were described frequently and at length by Ademar of Chabannes. But we now know that much of what Ademar wrote about this council was pure fiction, and his description of its Peace stipulations is so generic that some now doubt that it ever took place. Since the same writings of Ademar provide our only source for the Peace decrees of a council at Bourges also supposedly held in 1031, some doubt the reality of that council as well.[101] The councils of Poitiers pose even more difficulties. Most historians believe that the first was held sometime between 1000 and 1014, but its date cannot be further delimited from the three sources that attest it: a conciliar decree naming its bishops, a charter referring to the council, and a chronicle account clearly based on the charter and so not really an independent attestation.[102] Thomas Head believed that these three sources did not refer to a single council but to two separate ones. The one attested by the conciliar decrees was held ca. 1000, because the bishop of Périgord should have been present and was not, and the bishopric was vacant precisely in that year. The one attested by the charter and the chronicle was held ca. 1010/11. Arguing from a statement in Raoul Glaber's *Histories* and a hint in the conciliar decree, Head also believed that Aquitainian Peace councils were held every five years.[103] He therefore sought out evidence for additional Aquitainian Peace councils, finding it in charters issued by Duke William V of Aquitaine in the requisite years. Thus, Head proposed that there were declarations of the Peace at Poitiers in ca. 1000, 1010/11, 1015,[104] 1025,[105] 1029/30, and 1036.[106] However, Raoul Glaber's statement that oaths of Peace were to be renewed every five years comes in his account of the councils held at the time of the millennium of Christ's Passion (1033) not his Incarnation (1000). And most of the charters with which Head filled the gaps mention neither Peace councils nor any stipulations associated with the Peace, nor do they indicate the presence of large numbers of bishops. This stands in striking contrast to charters issued in association with the Peace of Anse in 994,[107] the Peace of Héry in 1024,[108] and the Peace of Poitiers ca. 1030.[109] All these charters refer explicitly to the Peace of God declared on the occasions the charters were issued; indeed, all appear to be performative applications to specific monasteries of the Peace just declared.

Such nagging little problems are actually of considerable importance. We have good, concrete sources for a dense cluster of Aquitainian Peace councils before 1000, after which their number appears to have declined markedly. If Head was correct, then the Peace of God remained a going concern even after 1000. If he was not (and he probably was not), how can we believe the Peace of God remained all that important after the first councils? In fact, it appears that the Peace was sputtering out until Oliba of Vic reinvigorated it by inventing the Truce of God in 1027.

The Truce of God presents its own difficulties, particularly in the north of the kingdom of France. There exist manuscripts of two important Peace decrees, one usually thought to be for the diocese of Laon, the other for the diocese of Cambrai. The latter is usually held to be the Peace declared by Bishop Gerard of Cambrai at Douai in 1034–35; the former is often tacitly assumed to be associated with Gerard's older contemporary Adalbero, bishop of Laon. Both were modelled on the Peace of Compiègne from 1023, itself modelled on the Peace of Verdun of ca. 1021–22. The difficulty is that both Peace texts are preceded by a declaration of the Truce of God. And Raoul Glaber explicitly stated that the Truce of God was not accepted in northern France until after 1041/42. Perhaps Raoul was wrong or has been misinterpreted. Perhaps the extant texts grafted a Truce of God onto earlier declarations of Peace at Laon and Douai. In any event, after 1041/42 evidence for the Truce of God does become common in northern France, making it likely that Raoul Glaber was correct: the Truce of God did face resistance there. It did not spread like wildfire throughout the kingdom after 1027. If so, the question becomes why it faced resistance: was it because of warfare between the king, Henry I, and the sons of Odo II of Blois, as Raoul says? Or was it because it was regarded as too radical and impossible to enforce? If the latter, what finally made the Truce acceptable? All historians have their opinions, but there is no consensus.[110]

Regional Inflections of the Peace of God

Many scholars argue that it is a mistake to see the Peace and Truce of God as a single, coherent program that spread irresistibly. Instead, as Thomas Head wrote, it was less a single movement than "a group of associated regional movements."[111] But this realization should not be taken to such an extreme that we lose sight of just how consistent and coherent the Peace and Truce were. As already mentioned, the Peace of Charroux was the basis for all subsequent declarations of the Peace for at least the next ten years, the first Peace of Poitiers actually referring to its acts in stipulating its own. This was only to be expected, given the overlap in the membership of the first councils. The same five episcopal sees were represented at Charroux,

Saint-Paulien, and Poitiers. Four bishops who attended Charroux also attended Limoges; three who attended Limoges attended Poitiers. Similarly, as just noted, the Peace of Verdun-sur-le-Doubs of ca. 1021–22 was the model for the Peace of Compiègne of 1023, which itself was the model for the Truce of God as established in Laon, Douai, Thérouanne, and Normandy: the same text, *Fratres karissimi*, is common to them all. The Peace of Vienne was probably declared around the same time as that of Verdun, since they are so similar to each other. And just as Verdun was the ultimate source of all later northern Peaces and Truces, so was Vienne for many subsequent southern renditions.

Given such conscious, purposeful borrowings, one cannot doubt that the Peace and later the Truce were seen as coherent programs. Nevertheless, it is also true that they entered different regions at different times under quite different political conditions. An extreme example is provided by the Truce of God initiated at Toulouges in 1027. Its sponsor was Oliba, bishop of Vic, abbot of Santa Maria de Ripoll and Saint-Michel de Cuxa, and brother of the count of Cerdanya. Strangely, in presiding over a council at Toulouges he was acting not in his own diocese but in that of Elne; nor was Toulouges at all a common location for a council. The reason appears to have been that Oliba and his family had interests in the village of Baho near Toulouges. His family had given it to Oliba's monastery of Cuxa, and under Oliba's leadership Cuxa had proceeded to buy up nearby lands, making the village one of its most important possessions. In issuing a Peace and Truce for the diocese of Elne, Oliba was really protecting an estate that his family had given to his own monastery.[112]

The Peace and Truce of God also served the political interests of rulers, whether princes or bishops. We have already seen how this might happen in one of the events that foreshadowed the Peace of God—the oaths of peace forced from the knights of the Velay by Bishop Wido of Le Puy around 975. Similar considerations were operating on a much larger scale when Wido organized a true Peace council at Le Puy around 994. Fortified by the example of Charroux, instead of acting solely on his own and for his own diocese as he had two decades earlier, Wido now organized a much larger council, attended by a number of unnamed "princes and nobles" and at least eight bishops from four different ecclesiastical provinces. None of the bishops had a position that would allow us to see them as "representing" their provinces (none, for example, were metropolitans). And the episcopal cities they ruled were scattered across a vast area—from Toulouse and Elne in the far southwest to Glandève in the far southeast to Clermont in the north of the Massif Central. The most notable thing about the attending bishops is that their sees did not include a single one from the territories ruled from Poitiers by the contemporary duke of Aquitaine, William IV Ironarm, even though his territories included sees in the provinces of Bourges and Bordeaux, some of whose suffragans did attend. Instead, Wido's council gathered together bishops who ruled within the vast regions that had been left "princeless" by the demise of the old Auvergnat dukes of Aquitaine and the growing powerlessness of the margraves of Gothia at Toulouse. Within this vacuum arose a welter of effectively autonomous viscounties. The result was not so much feudal anarchy in the sense of unrestrained violence (though there were plenty of small-scale armed actions). The real problem was the absence of any structured forum within which political decisions could be made—in the Toulousain, the Narbonnais, the Viennois, and the Velay itself. The response of Wido and his colleagues was to provide what was lacking: a forum within which the powerful could come together to make agreements that would regulate their actions during conflicts and would be binding because they had agreed to and sworn to them.

In Aquitaine itself, ruled from Poitiers, the situation was a little different. Although the authority of the dukes was recognized in theory, its limits were constantly tested. Even in Poitou and the Limousin their most important men used alliances offered by the counts of Anjou to stalemate the dukes' efforts at control. As a result, the dukes of Aquitaine were able to manage their unruly nobles only by setting some against others and by constantly campaigning and negotiating.[113] Their sponsorship of the Peace of God was another weapon in their arsenal. In fact, the very first Peace council was held in the midst of the best known of the Aquitainian wars, that between the viscounts of Limoges (allied to Duke William IV Ironarm and his ally Count Odo I of Blois) and the lords of La Marche (allied to Count Fulk Nerra of Anjou, rival of William IV and committed enemy of Odo). And it was held at Charroux, in the court of the castle, right in the heart of La Marche next to the famous monastery of which the lord of La Marche was advocate and where he would be buried. William himself was not present, perhaps because it would have been too great a provocation to Boso of La Marche. But he was certainly aware of and supportive of the bishops' actions, since immediately afterwards they hastened to Poitiers to make a report.[114] And the duke's leadership, alongside his bishops, of subsequent Peace assemblies at Limoges and Poitiers was absolutely clear. Concerning the latter, a charter attests to his presence at the council as "monarch of all Aquitaine," while the council's acts explicitly stated that he had summoned it.[115] The 994 Council of Limoges took place against the backdrop of a ravaging disease (usually identified as ergotism). Ademar's accounts of it also foregrounded the duke's leadership, as the bishops took his counsel in declaring a three-day fast and the duke himself summoned the people and nobles "subject to his rule" to attend. The charter attesting the Peace at Poitiers (1029–30) described the council's participants in terms that reflected the ideal order of society: the king (Robert the Pious) ruling the entire kingdom justly, Duke William VI acting under his rule, then the bishops and priests and all orders of clergy holding councils attended by "a countless multitude of the people, both nobles and poor." But when it came to enforcing the terms of the Peace, that was done by the duke himself, in a judgement against corrupt judges and provosts preying on the inhabitants of the lands of Saint-Maixent.[116] In fact, whether or not they issued declarations of the Peace of God, more large public assemblies of mixed religious and political import were held under William V the Great of Aquitaine than any other contemporary French prince (save the king himself), most famously on the occasion of the elevation of the newly discovered head of John the Baptist at Angély in 1016.[117]

In other words, the dukes of Aquitaine, William V especially, promoted events that showed them acting in regalian fashion, not in competition with the king but mimetically adopting a king's attributes as a model for their own by summoning and presiding over councils that brought all their subjects together, lay and religious, greater and lesser, all social and ecclesiastical orders. And perhaps the most essential of their duties as duke was responsibility for the peace and protection of the poor and defenceless against the violence of the powerful. Sponsoring the Peace of God allowed William V to appear alongside the bishops of his duchy, exercising the kind of authority that God gave only to princes and prelates to curb the so-called "rapacity" of castellans that caused him such trouble.

The Peace in Burgundy was different yet again. The duchy had been subjugated by King Robert the Pious in two stages, first the south in 1005, then the north in 1016. Robert's victory required several long sieges, but it was achieved mostly through negotiations with regional leaders. The negotiations eventually produced a complicated political solution. First, the king was not allowed to rule Burgundy directly. Instead, the Burgundian leadership permitted his son to rule as duke. Second, the regional leadership of Burgundy was left largely intact. The Peace of God that Robert sponsored in Burgundy set the seal on the accommodation. Its imposition was administered by Robert's chief lieutenant in Burgundy—Hugh, bishop of Auxerre and count of Chalon. It was established by councils in all the leading political centres of the duchy: Verdun-sur-le-Doubs (in Hugh's county of Chalon), Héry (near Auxerre), Dijon (the centre of the stoutest resistance to Robert), and Beaune (midway between Auxerre and Dijon and a viscounty crucial to Robert's takeover). Though Robert was present at Héry, he was not mentioned as directly involved in any of the other councils. Even at Héry his activities were not singled out by our sources—this in striking contrast to the way Aquitainian sources call attention to William V's leadership of the Peace. But such reticence was itself a perfect expression of the Burgundian settlement, according to which Robert ruled distantly and indirectly only, leaving Burgundians to rule themselves under the aegis of his son and lieutenant. It was a regime of local, consensual government entailing local, consensual commitments to a Peace.[118]

One could cite other examples of the Peace (and Truce) of God being tailored to the specific needs of localities and their leaderships. For example, the Truce was probably first introduced into Normandy in the 1040s during the minority of William II. Here, the Norman bishops appear to have used the program to buttress a young duke's authority and legitimacy.[119] Yet recognizing regional variations in the implementation of the program does not really answer a fundamental question; it only draws attention to the fact that it has not been answered. Why were the Peace and Truce appealing to so many different leaders in the late tenth and early eleventh centuries? Why could Robert the Pious and William V of Aquitaine see them as useful to their needs? Why could bishops of so many different dioceses and abbots of monasteries see them as useful to theirs? Not least, what was the benefit to the lords and knights who agreed to swear the oaths?

Legislation and Lordship

The single most important way in which the Peace of God differed from Carolingian capitularies about peace is that the Peace of God was good legislation. This assertion might seem implausible. Scholars frequently cite Carolingian "legislation" (capitularies and conciliar decrees) as precedents for the Peace of God. And the Peace has often been seen not as legislation at all but as a religious movement led by bishops trying to fill the vacuum left by the decline of Carolingian-style royal power who therefore relied on religious sanctions (primarily excommunication) to enforce the agreements. Nevertheless, the assertion remains true.[120]

One should begin with the differences between Carolingian capitularies on peace and the articles of the Peace of God. As is well known, capitularies are very difficult to define as a genre. They are frequently referred to as legislation, and many do present rules of law or administration. But just as many are exhortations to moral, ethical, Christian, and politically upright action. This was as true for Alcuin's contributions to the *Admonitio generalis* (the first great capitulary) as it was for Hincmar of Reims's phrasings in the capitulary of Ver (the last). But it is really

Hincmar who is crucial to consider in this regard. He has a reputation among historians as an authoritative voice whose positions represented the most developed formulation of Carolingian legislation on peace and church property, and he wrote a massive number of tracts and several collections of precedents that might have passed on these positions to the tenth century. And so it is his writings and the capitularies in whose drafting he participated that are most frequently mined by scholars seeking to document the Carolingian foundations of the Peace of God.[121] Yet if we turn to the first Peace council, Charroux, we find little echo of Hincmar's rhetoric and none of his favourite citations. Instead, in the very manuscript that transmits Charroux's canons, we find a source of precedents very different from Hincmar: selections from early Frankish episcopal councils at Orléans, Arles, and Chalon, and selections from the *Statuta ecclesiae antiqua* (a collection of canons from early Gallic councils). There are also a few canons taken from earlier councils that cannot be identified. One of them provides a definition of "a sacrilegious" as a person who has committed the kinds of actions prohibited by the Peace of God: attacks on clerics of any sort and the taking away from their houses, fields, and vineyards of gold, silver, vestments, grain, or wine. All such acts are to be punished by an excommunication, which is also phrased in the language used by the Peace councils: he shall be "ejected from the thresholds of the church," "held outside the thresholds of the church," "unless he does satisfaction with penance."[122]

Charroux and the other early Peace councils were assemblies of Aquitainian bishops renewing contact with the legislation produced during the heroic age of Aquitainian bishops. In their own minds, the precedents for their actions were Gallic, not Carolingian. And so Hincmar's capitularies, conciliar pronouncements, and tracts almost certainly provided no precedent for the articles of the early Peace councils. One can tell this simply by examining the legislation itself. Take, for example, Hincmar's treatise known as *De raptoribus*, which figures as an appendix to the capitulary of Quierzy in 857. Some 1,000 words long, it offers a collection of quotations from the prophets, the gospels, Paul's epistles, Gregory the Great, and Pseudo-Isidore, joined together by typical Hincmarian jeremiad: "Let them hear what the prophet Isaiah said ... Let the thieves and plunderers hear what the prophet also said ... Let them hear what St. Paul the Apostle said ..."[123] For Carloman's capitulary of Ver, Hincmar wrote a 500-word prologue denouncing *rapinae et depraedationes* as a poison that had infected the body and the soul, which was why the kingdom had fallen under the domination of pagans and foreigners; for "how can we defeat our enemies when the blood of our brothers drips from our mouth and our hands are covered with blood and our arms are weighed down with the miseries we have caused and the fruits of our plunder ...?"[124] Rhetoric of this sort was not absent from the Peace of God. It is hinted at in the hagiographical accounts of miracles performed before the crowds that attended the assemblies, in the language of the letter that some bishops claimed had fallen from heaven, and in the sermons of Ademar of Chabannes and the *Histories* of Raoul Glaber. However, it is not present in the articles of the Peace of God themselves. The stipulations of the Peace from Charroux are recorded in just three short articles. In their brevity and concrete focus they are far more reminiscent of sixth-century Gallic councils than of the later West Frankish Councils of Fismes and Trosly. The entirety of the Peace of Narbonne in 1054 is twenty-nine short articles totalling approximately 1,500 words, and this is a relatively long Peace text.[125] And the difference is not just a matter of length. The articles of the

Peace councils are crisp, clear, to the point, and eminently practical. This is evident in the canons of Charroux and Le Puy quoted above, but it remained true of all Peace and Truce councils. Article 3 of the Council of Narbonne, for example, is simply a listing of feast days and periods of the year, followed by:

> Let no Christian harm any other Christian or presume to mistreat him or despoil him of property.

Article 6 reads:

> If anyone does any injury or harm to anyone else, by the judgement of his own bishop or those clerics to whom the bishop will commit the matter he shall do right according to his degree of guilt by the judgement of cold water or by exile, as has been established.

Article 7:

> Whoever wishes to build a castle or fortification at the approach of Lent, Ascension, Pentecost, or Advent, which are [the periods of] the Truce of God, he shall not be allowed to do so unless he begins the work two weeks before the said periods and this is made known publicly.

There is also this sampling from the Compiègne oath of 1023:

> I will not break into a church in any manner.
>
> I will not violate the precinct (*salvamentum*) that contains the storehouses within the circuit surrounding a church, save on account of a malefactor who has broken this peace either by committing homicide or by seizing a man or a horse.
>
> And if for these reasons I do violate the area of the store-houses, I will knowingly take away nothing from them except that malefactor or his surety.
>
> I will not attack a cleric or a monk not bearing worldly arms nor those travelling with them without lance and shield; nor

> will I seize their horse unless in they are in the act of committing an offense so that I have legal cause to do so, or unless they will not amend such an offense within fifteen days after I have given them notice.

> I will not seize steers, cows, pigs, sheep, lambs, goats, or asses, nor the loads they carry, nor mares and their unbroken colts.[126]

In complete contrast to Carolingian capitularies and conciliar decrees, articles of the Peace of God state clearly and simply not only what one cannot do but also what one can do and under what circumstances. Equally important, they are not phrased as the command of a distant ruler who demands obedience nor as the moral injunction of bishops transmitting the imprecations of prophets and apostles. They are stipulations agreed to by those who have sworn the oath of Peace, who are regulating their own actions.

As stipulations agreed to by the participants themselves, the constitutions of the Peace (the early ones especially) also hint at processes of negotiation and compromise that produced the articles. In other words, the councils were producing real legislation. They were not trying to construct an ideal society in terms of broad religious precepts; they dealt with concrete realities as experienced in practice. This is one reason Peace articles are often hard for us to understand: they used terms that had developed technically precise meanings which contemporaries knew but which we no longer do. The Peace of Compiègne (and the many Peaces related to it) allowed the physical seizure of the person who had violated the Peace agreements, but they also allowed the seizure of "his surety" (*warnamentum*)—that is, a person who had been publicly named a guarantor of an individual's oath-bound engagement, so that any legal action (including seizure of person and property) made to enforce the engagement could be made against the guarantor if his party did not satisfy the terms. Or take this article, also from Compiègne:

> I will not take (*prendam*) a male or female serf (*villanum, villanam*) or servants (*servientes*) or merchants (*mercatores*) nor will I take (*tollam*) their money, nor will I make them redeem (*redimere*), nor will I take (*tollam*) their goods so that they lose [them] on account of the war of their lord (*werram senioris sui*), nor will I beat them for their belongings.

Measured against modern ideas of "peace," this engagement seems incongruous, to say the least. But its very incongruities make it an ideal entry point for understanding not only what the Peace of God really was but also its purpose and the reasons it can be judged successful within those limits. The word here translated as "war" (*werra*) referred to a legitimate, publicly declared and acknowledged state of armed conflict between two lords. It is often translated as "feud," which is appropriate as long as it is recalled that a feud was not mere "private" vengeance but a legally recognized and formally publicized state of enmity. The conflict between the lords of Périgord and La Marche that lay in the background of the Peace of Charroux was a *werra*; and although personal hatreds and vengeance for personal affronts were certainly part of it, it was also fought for control of territory and public jurisdiction over territory and subjects.[127] Since it was public warfare and not private vengeance, those involved in a *werra* were not restricted to attacking only the persons who had wronged them. They could attack their lands and seize their belongings. In this context, it is important to realize that in the above article two of the Latin terms (*villanus/villana, servientes*) explicitly—and a third (*mercatores*) implicitly—denoted classes of persons regarded as property of the enemy lord and therefore legitimately open to capture during *werrae*, just as much as his own castle. As for the Latin *redimere*, the word is often translated as "ransom," but in modern English "ransom" is usually associated with violent kidnapping and profiteering, which was not necessarily at issue here. Rather, throughout the entire Middle Ages, if one individual were legally owed anything by another (a debt, a fine, a service) and its payment was not forthcoming, then after a public declaration the claimant had the right to seize the person who owed the obligation (or his surety or his property) and hold what he had taken until the obligation was fulfilled and the failure of fulfilment compensated for. This was not ransom; it was "redemption." In Peaces like those of Compiègne, peasants, servants, and conveyors were being held in this fashion until they could redeem themselves, either for their own actions and obligations or for those of their lord.

In trying to understand such actions, one must keep in mind a constant principle of all medieval law, what might be called its "performative" basis.[128] If one claimed a right—the right to take timber from a wood or fish from a stream or tolls on a road—one had to actually exercise that right and *be seen* exercising it. Proof that one's claims were legally valid would be met by producing witnesses who could publicly attest that they had *seen* the rights being exercised (for example, the timber being cut down and hauled out or the peasants paying *census* to the claimant or his agents). Conversely, if one disputed these claims, one had to be seen publicly *resisting* these actions, including by attacking those doing the taking, receiving, and hauling; and these acts of resistance would also be publicly witnessed, allowing the witnesses to assert that the opposing side did *not* lawfully exercise those rights. This is one reason why disputes over rights (including rights over people) often involved public acts of taking and forcible resistance to the taking. That, in turn, is why ecclesiastical sources of the period were so often built around narratives of violence.

What the Peace of God did was set limits to actions during legitimate wars and disputes. Its intention was not to end *werrae* but to restrict the range of persons and places subject to their harm. That is what made the Peace good legislation. It did not try for the impossible (as did Carolingian capitularies). It aimed at the achievable.

Similar considerations underlay another set of stipulations common in Peace agreements. Again to quote from the oath of Compiègne:

> I will not destroy a mill nor seize the grain in it unless I will
> be *in cavallicata* or *in hoste*, and unless it will be on my land.

The two italicized phrases here may have been vernacular and Latin terms for the same thing or slightly different varieties of something similar (the latter a major campaign including foot soldiers, the former an expedition of mounted warriors only), but the essential agreement was this: one could legitimately seize grain in mills when one was on a formal, military expedition as long as one took it from one's own lands which legitimately owed such requisitions. Here Magnou-Nortier's interpretation is extremely helpful. The "evil customs" (*malae consuetudines*) so often denounced in monastic writings of the period were recognized exactions of lordship. "Customs" were not "evil" in and of themselves. *Consuetudines* was simply a common word for legitimate exactions by or on behalf of rulers, many of them having to do with requisitions that supported wars, sieges, and the construction, garrisoning, and defence of castles. What made a custom "evil" was that it was exacted from the wrong people in the wrong place at the wrong time in the wrong amount. This was often the case with many of the actions prohibited by the Peace of God. The goal was not to outlaw seizures of peasant belongings for redemption or requisitions from peasants for military needs. The goal was to regulate them. And the most important such regulation was this: any number of acts of lordship were valid when made on one's own dependents, one's own lands, or lands on which one had the right to make such claims. On all other lands and from all other persons, they were illegitimate.

Hence, the importance of what might be called "*nisi*" clauses in articles of the Peace: the swearer promised not to commit this or that action "unless" certain conditions applied. A typical example is the above article prohibiting the seizure of grain from mills "unless I will be on caval-cade or on campaign and unless it will be on my land." But there were many others. Merchants and pilgrims were not to be attacked *unless* they were being seized for com-mitting a crime. Noble women and women travelling with them would not be attacked *unless* they were in the act of committing harm to the swearer. Castles could not be built within the period of the Truce *unless* the work had begun at least two weeks before the Truce began. No one should violate a church or the buildings within its protected perimeter *except* for the bishop or his immediate agent when collecting unpaid rent. No one should violate such buildings and spaces *unless* a fortification had been built within the perimeter and the fortification was being used to launch raids and store plunder. No one was to seize the property of a serf (*villanus*), *but* the serf himself might be seized *as long as* the seizure was done by law and it was for the serf's own misdeed, not the misdeed of his lord.

The Peace of God was therefore not a repudiation of lordship. It was a regulation of lordship that implicitly accepted lords' rights. It was the result of negotiations and compromises that worked out how lordships could coexist. One already sees this at Anse in 994. Some doubt that this was a true Peace assembly, for as they have been trans-mitted to us its decrees address the reform of religious life (including the laity's) rather than the categories of the

Peace of God. Yet our two sources for the council—one charter for Cluny and one for Saint-Barnard of Romans—leave little doubt that it was a Peace council. Both charters mention "peace" as one of the council's primary concerns. Both threaten "violators" of the decrees with anathema (the usual sanction of Peace decrees). Most decisive of all are the terms of Cluny's charter, issued in the name of the council's bishops. It singled out twenty-two monasteries, churches, and estates of Cluny (plus the burg of Cluny itself) and placed them under protection of what is immediately recognizable as the Peace. The churches, their tithes, their services, and the burg of Cluny were exempt from all illegitimate entry and seizure, using the vocabulary of the Peace of God (*infringere, violare, predam auferre*). The bishops further stipulated that no "public judge," "collector," count, or army could erect a fortification of any sort within the burg of Cluny and the other named locations. Finally, they decreed that no one of any secular standing or military office could make any seizure (*predam auferre*) from the men and territory of the castle and burg of Cluny and Charlieu, including steers, cows, pigs, horses—these the usual categories of animals named in Peace decrees.[129]

In the end, the important issue is not whether Anse was or was not a Peace council. The important issue is that in 994 the categories of the Peace of God were already being used to define Cluny's exclusive lordship to its core estates. Equally important is the converse, unstated but implicit in Cluny's charter and explicit in later Peace decrees: what lords could *not* do on estates within Cluny's lordship they *could* do on lands subject to their own lordship. This is why lords supported the restrictions imposed by the Peace of God. It is also why the Peace of God was useful to and promoted by William the Great in Aquitaine, Robert the Pious in Burgundy, and the consortia of bishops and lords acting on their own, without princely guidance, throughout the French Midi: the Peace of God provided rulers with a way of regulating the inevitable proliferation of lordships throughout their territories in a way that did not require them to have the power to enforce decrees (a power they did not have), because enforcement relied on the self-interested decisions of the lords themselves, whether those lords were bishops and abbots or counts and castellans.

The Peace Militias

The Peace of God consisted of a set of oaths by which individuals promised not to engage in certain kinds of activity. But exactly who swore the oaths? And how were violations sanctioned? The questions go to the heart of debates about the nature of the Peace and its change over time. In an important article Thomas Bisson made a distinction between the "sanctified" Peace of the early movement, the "instituted" Peace that developed in a second stage, and the "organized" or "institutionalized" Peace that developed later.[130] Bisson established his typology around the different ways the oaths of Peace were enforced. In effect, for Bisson the "sanctified peace" depended on passing moments of religious fervour that mobilized large masses of the population. It developed no institutional mechanism to enforce its oaths. Its only real sanction was the excommunication of those who violated their oaths and broke the terms of the Peace. It was a very weak, undependable sanction. The one notable exception only proved the failure of a program based on oaths: the so-called "Peace league of Bourges."

Its story is told in two narrative sources whose accounts differ sharply. The more famous was written by Andrew, a monk of Fleury (Saint-Benoît-sur-Loire), in his continuation of the *Miracles* of St. Benedict, Fleury's patron saint. According to Andrew, in 1038 Archbishop Aimo of Bourges gathered the bishops of his province and convinced them to establish a Peace in each of their dioceses. One of the oath's stipulations committed participants to attack militarily those who violated the Peace:

> I promise to move with all my forces (*totis viribus*) against those who dare transgress these decrees and to not give up until the aim of the transgressor is overcome.

Aimo and his bishops further agreed that this oath would be required of every male in their dioceses fifteen years of age and older. On the basis of this commitment Aimo was able to assemble militias consisting of "a multitude of the people." In Andrew's account the militias were at first remarkably successful. Marching behind the banners of churches like "another Israelite people," they attacked and razed the castles of "rebels" against the Peace, until the mere news of their approach caused seasoned, well-armed garrisons to open the gates of their strongholds and flee before "the multitude of unarmed people" (*multitudo inermis vulgi*). But Andrew was a monk presenting an *exemplum*, a morality tale. The archbishop's success led to ambition, which led to a fall. Aimo and "a multitude of the people of Bourges" attacked the castle of one Stephen and burned it to the ground. Over 1,400 men and women died, since nearby peasants had taken refuge within it, seeking safety from the horde. Stephen was one of the few who escaped, though he was captured and imprisoned at Bourges. The crime brought down God's vengeance. When Aimo next attacked Odo, lord of Déols, on the River Cher, his forces were massacred, including, says Andrew, 500 clerics.[131]

What Andrew does not tell us is that Odo of Déols was one of the two most powerful lords in the archdiocese of Bourges; the other was Archbishop Aimo's own brother, the lord of Bourbon. We do not have to imagine how Odo's side would have told the story; we have their version, in a brief narrative found in a set of annals from the monastery of Déols itself. It says nothing about the Peace of God or a Peace militia composed of "the multitude of unarmed people." Instead, it begins with a battle over the castle of Châteauneuf. In the course of that conflict, Odo of Déol's son Ebbo was killed by Geoffrey, Archbishop Aimo's viscount at Bourges. Aimo and Geoffrey then attacked Odo, leading to the battle on the Cher, where "the Lord fought marvellously for Odo" and crushed his enemies. The archbishop escaped, wounded. Another son of Odo soon retook the castle of Châteauneuf.[132]

Putting these two accounts together, it would be easy to conclude that the battle on the Cher was nothing but a bloody moment in an ongoing feud. It would also be easy to conclude that Aimo, his brother, and his viscount cynically used the Peace to recruit an army and lend legitimacy to their campaign.[133] But it is unlikely that this is how Aimo saw it. Bourges was a major metropolitan see and the capital of the region known as the Berry. However, since at least 923 the Berry had been divided into separate political districts. Upper Berry, centred on Bourges, tended to ally with the kings to the north. Lower Berry tended to ally with the Auvergnat dukes of Aquitaine and the motley of princes who succeeded them. The recognized leaders of lower Berry were the lords of Déols. Châteauneuf was their most strategically important castle, guarding the approach from Bourges. What lay behind the Peace league of Bourges and the battles over Déols and Châteauneuf was the effort of the archbishops and viscounts to restore the authority of Bourges over the entirety of the *pagus*. From their point of view, the Peace militia was not fighting a "private" war. It was the army of the archdiocese acting to extend the metropolitan see's rightful authority over its territory and subjects. Of course, Odo and Stephen saw matters differently. But approaching Andrew's account with this interpretation in mind, we notice an important aspect of the conflict. The fault of Odo and Stephen was not that they did not obey the stipulations of the Peace by committing rapine and plunder. Their fault was that they would not swear the Peace oath in the first place. That is what made them "rebels" against it.

The Peace league of Bourges is yet another demonstration of the way princes and prelates used the Peace of God to assert their authority within a regime of castles. Indeed, the Peace allowed them to remake their authority so that secular and even military power became ever more infused with religious sanction and meaning. But the event also reflects a developing transformation of the Peace of God. First, Aimo's Peace was essentially a decree. Andrew of Fleury implicitly defined it as such, writing that Aimo "constrained" oaths (*constringit*) from every male fifteen years and older. This is what Bisson meant by an "instituted" Peace. Second, by demanding the oath from all adult males and not just lords and their warriors, Aimo raised an army to enforce both membership in the Peace association and respect for its terms. Both are often thought to have been innovations designed to put teeth into the flaccid sanction of excommunication that had hitherto been the only real mechanism for enforcing the oaths of the Peace of God.

Were these aspects of the Peace of Bourges really new? As with nearly every important question about the program, it is hard to know. In the proto-Peace of Le Puy of ca. 975, oaths were first "requested" by Bishop Wido. When his request was refused he summoned the armies of his nephews and forced the oaths on the unwilling. Thus, even before the Peace of God was the Peace of God, it was "constrained" under threat of arms by a bishop who himself exercised comital powers and whose nephews commanded armies as neighbouring counts. We know few details about the Peace of Charroux in 989; but the acts as extant describe its anathemas as a "decree" of its bishops. The bishops meeting at Anse in 994 issued rulings on a host of matters both secular and ecclesiastical; but one that closely resembles a Peace stipulation they issued as a conciliar decision (*statuerunt*). The stipulations of the Peace of Le Puy in 994 were introduced as an admonition (*ammonemus*) but summarized as an *institutio*. The bishops who met Poitiers under the duke of Aquitaine (ca. 1000–ca. 1014) introduced their primary Peace regulations as a decision (*constituerunt*) and an establishment (*instituerunt*). According to the *Gesta episcoporum Autissidorensium*, the bishop of Auxerre "established" (*constituit*) an assembly of bishops, nobles, and people to restore and swear peace. One of the oaths that resulted (Verdun-sur-les-Doubs) described its myriad terms as "ordered" (*praecipimus*). In the Peace and Truce of Toulouges in 1027, the first set of stipulations was presented as a decision of the assembled bishops, clergy, and people (*constituerunt*), but the second set was presented as commands and prohibitions by the bishops and clergy alone (*precipimus, interdicimus*). The bishops who met at Saint-Gilles in 1041 or 1042 termed their Peace as a *definitio* and *decretum*. One could adduce many more examples, but these should suffice to show that the Peace had always in some sense been "instituted." There could be negotiation over its terms, more or less implicit or overt coercion. But the Peace and Truce were presented as a slate of stipulations, a *constitutio* or *institutio*. Even so, one must remember that within the West Frankish tradition the whole point of a language of peace and assembly was to mask dissension and coercion by expressing decisions as the collective unanimity of individual wills.[134] And the oaths sworn by those who gave their agreement to the constitutions of the Peace were not a sham. They were vital to its legitimacy. In any event, there was no great innovation either at Bourges in 1038 or at Narbonne in 1054 (which Barthélemy holds to have been the first Peace or Truce established as an "ordinance").[135] Instead, what seems to have happened is this: as the Peace and Truce developed, their terms became increasingly regularized until they formed a consistent, recognized "program" that could be "instituted" with various amendments and changes according to circumstances.

A harder question to answer is whether Aimo of Bourges innovated in demanding oaths from all males fifteen and older and in making their oaths the basis of service in a militia to enforce the Peace. One reason his demands have seemed so innovative is because so many scholars have held that the only sanction of the early Peace and Truce was excommunication. Certainly our sources consistently emphasize excommunication as the primary sanction for violators of the Peace. But is that not to be expected? The articles of the Peace were most often established in councils represented as being held under the authority of bishops, this being true even when dukes, counts, other lay lords, and "the people" were mentioned as playing an important role at them. And excommunication was, of course, the primary sanction of episcopal decrees—the bishops' "spiritual sword" that complemented the "secular sword" of lay authorities. But there is a deeper issue here: it is simply not true that excommunication was the only sanction of the early oaths of Peace.[136] Nor is it true that such excommunication worked as a sanction only when people feared eternal damnation, the less pious being willing to ignore it. A number of councils took great care to define exactly what the effects of excommunication were; a few took even greater care to define the differences between excommunication and anathema.[137] And eternal damnation was the threat only for anathema—a greater spiritual penalty imposed only for those who refused to obey the strictures of the Peace even after they had been excommunicated. Ordinary excommunication was first and foremost a social penalty. Persons excommunicated could not attend mass and could not be buried in sacred ground. No masses could be said for their redemption. No Christian could eat, drink, or speak with them. The social purpose of this kind of excommunication was to put pressure on an individual from their family, friends, and all those with whom they might do business.[138] The purpose of the pressure was to force the individual to make amends for whatever acts of violence he had committed. Making amends meant doing penance in order to receive absolution and be restored to the community of the faithful. But it also meant making legal amends—normally restoration of property taken or its value and/or some form of monetary compensation. The requirement was articulated clearly in Peace programs during and after the 1030s, especially in the south of France and Catalonia. Thus, at Vic in 1033 those who violated the Peace were required to make amends within fifteen days, after which they would have to amend double the amount (the additional amount to be divided between the bishop and the count). Those who violated the Truce by any harmful act short of homicide would pay double compensation to the victim after paying a double fine to the bishop. Similar stipulations were made at Arles around 1040 and at Narbonne in 1054.[139] But such requirements were not unknown in the north of the kingdom, for around the same time the Peaces of Douai, Thérouanne, and Caen also required violators to pay a legal amend for their actions.[140]

There were other sanctions besides excommunication designed to put pressure on those who violated Peace regulations. A number of statutes mandated exile for those who killed someone during the period of the Truce, including those of Caen and Vic.[141] If we can judge by later practices, such exile was less a punishment than a practical attempt to reduce the danger of vengeance killings by removing a potential target of retaliation from the area until the parties could reach a settlement.[142] In the 1030s, the Peace of Amiens and Corbie required the principals involved in any serious dispute to come before the bishop and count of Amiens, in order to try for a peaceful settlement before the parties engaged in acts of hostility against each other.[143] The Peace declared at Poitiers in 1029–30 was immediately followed by a series of judicial assemblies under William VI of Aquitaine. The record of one of them survives: it seems almost a public, performative application of the Peace of God's protection of churches, because it required the very nobles of the region who would have just sworn the oaths to enforce the terms of the Peace in favour of the monastery of Saint-Maixent.[144]

A number of important Peace agreements required those swearing the oaths to name hostages who would be subject to all the hazards of law and *werra* if those for whom they stood surety failed in their obligations. This was already the case in one of the earliest. Around or soon after 1000, the Peace of Poitiers established that if anyone accused another over property claims that might lead to forcible seizures, the parties were to appear before "the prince of that region or the judge of the *pagus*" and receive a formal judicial hearing. If a party refused to do so, the prince or judge could seize the hostages. If the prince or judge found himself unable to execute justice, he was to summon the princes and bishops who had established the Peace, "and all as one would act for the destruction and harm" of the intransigeant until he accepted a judicial hearing.[145] Very similar enforcement procedures are intimated in the series of Peace oaths that derived from that of Verdun-sur-le-Doubs. All required the swearers to appoint hostages. All prohibited attacks on churches, the unarmed, and their properties and belongings. But all made an exception. In the words of Verdun: "except for that man who violates this peace."[146]

So the Peace and Truce of God did establish punishments and means of enforcement besides excommunication. Excommunication is more visible to us because that was the sanction available to the bishops who crafted the texts. But always excommunication was regarded, in practice, as a complement and inducement to mediation and judicial settlement; and in many cases, the Peace oaths presumed that military action would be taken against those who violated the oaths or would not swear them.

There remains the question of who normally swore the oaths. Even the seeming clarity of the case of Bourges becomes murkier when one begins to seriously consider its ramifications. Did all males fifteen years of age and older really swear Aimo's oath? Certainly not, for one cannot imagine the unfree being allowed to swear it or participate in the armed expeditions of the militia. So perhaps only all free adult males swore the oath. But that is not really a helpful distinction, since one of the period's hallmarks was the simultaneous insistence on a clear legal divide between free and unfree, and the difficulty of drawing the line in specific cases.[147] Sources issuing from other Peace assemblies are often equally problematic. Too often they are vague right where we need them to be precise, in part because their authors wanted to depict the assemblies as moments of social harmony and collective unanimity. As we saw at the beginning of this chapter, this tendency was especially pronounced in monastic sources, particularly hagiographies, which consistently refer to vast crowds of lay persons of both sexes and all statuses. All the more reason, then, to take the account of one monk seriously: in describing the Peace of Limoges (ca. 994), Ademar of Chabannes stated that it was sworn "by the dukes and princes."[148] The notice publishing the Peace of Le Puy (ca. 994), issued in the name of Bishop Wido of Le Puy, named the bishops who attended "and many princes and nobles, in countless numbers."[149] The acts of the assembly instituting the Peace of Poitiers (ca. 1000) spoke of the Peace being confirmed by "the duke and other princes."[150] The Peace of Vic (1033) begins: "This is the peace confirmed by bishops and abbots and counts and viscounts and other magnates and other God-fearing Christians." Yet when one reads the decrees of Vic, one senses that even these other Christians did not include freemen, let alone commoners, since the articles only raised issues that concerned a warrior aristocracy.[151] This is even truer of the Peaces of Vienne and Verdun and those descending from them: the stipulations make no sense unless they were sworn only by members of the military elite. A note appended to the oath of Verdun says as much: "We only order that this oath be sworn by those who are horsemen and who bear secular arms."[152]

It would therefore appear that Aimo of Bourges really did do something unheard of in demanding oaths from a broad swathe of the adult male population and in making their oaths the basis of an obligation to serve in a militia that would enforce not just the oaths but membership in Peace associations throughout his archdiocese. Furthermore, Andrew of Fleury tells us that this same oath was sworn not just in the archdiocese of Bourges but in all the dioceses of the province.[153] If true, that would mean that Aimo's Peace extended far into the Languedoc, including dioceses where we find references to near-contemporary Peace councils for which no acts survive (as at Mende, Rodez, Cahors, and Albi). We are on the way to a much different Peace of God, one that has interested historians less than the first decades of the movement but which was, if anything, even more important.

Notes

[68] Rodulfus Glaber, 4.9–16, pp. 184–97.

[69] Richard Landes, "Rodolfus Glaber and the Dawn of the New Millennium: Eschatology, Historiography, and the Year 1000," *Revue Mabillon* 68, n.s. 7 (1996): 57–77; Landes, "The Fear of an Apocalyptic Year 1000: Augustinian Historiography, Medieval and Modern," *Speculum* 75 (2000): 97–145; Landes, "The Birth of Heresy: A Millennial Phenomenon," *The Journal of Religious Studies* 24 (2000): 26–43. Contra: R. I. Moore, "The Birth of Popular Heresy: A Millennial Phenomenon?," *The Journal of Religious History* 24 (2000): 8–25.

[70] Justin Lake, *Richer of Saint-Rémi: The Methods and Mentality of a Tenth-Century Historian* (Washington, DC: The Catholic University of America Press, 2013).

[71] Barthélemy, *L'An mil*, p. 30.

[72] Dominique Iogna-Prat, *Agni immaculati: Recherches sur les sources hagiographiques relatives à Saint Maieul de Cluny (954–994)* (Paris: Éditions du Cerf, 1988); Iogna-Prat, "The Dead in the Celestial Bookkeeping of the Cluniac Monks Around the Year 1000," in *Debating the Middle Ages: Issues and Readings*, ed. Lester Little and Barbara Rosenwein (Oxford: Blackwell, 1998), pp. 340–62.

[73] Richard Landes, *Relics, Apocalypse, and the Deceits of History: Ademar of Chabannes, 989–1034* (Cambridge, MA: Harvard University Press, 1995).

[74] Barthélemy, *L'An mil*, pp. 140–42.

[75] Bernhard Töpfer, *Volk und Kirche zur Zeit der beginnenden Gottesfriedensbewegung in Frankreich* (Berlin: Rütten & Loening, 1957); Richard Landes, "Between Aristocracy and Heresy: Popular Participation in the Limousin Peace of God, 994–1033," in *The Peace of God*, ed. Head and Landes, pp. 184–218.

[76] Abbo of Fleury, *Liber apologeticus ad Hugonem et Rodbertum reges Francorum*, PL 139:461–72 at 471–72; Barthélemy, *L'An mil*, pp. 143–44.

[77] Einar Joranson, "The Great German Pilgrimage of 1064–1065," in *The Crusades and Other Historical Essays Presented to Dana C. Munro by his Former Students*, ed. Louis J. Paetow (New York: F. S. Crofts, 1928), pp. 3–43, with references, especially to Meyer von Knonau's *Jahrbücher*.

[78] David C. Van Meter, "Apocalyptic Moments and the Eschatological Rhetoric of Reform in the Early Eleventh Century: The Case of the Visionary of St. Vaast," in *The Apocalyptic Year 1000: Religious Expectation and Social Change, 950–1050*, ed. Richard Landes

et al. (Oxford: Oxford University Press, 2003), pp. 311–25 at 316.

[79] *GEC*, 3.52, p. 485.

[80] Hippolyte Delehaye, S. J., "Note sur la légende de la lettre du Christ tombée du ciel," *Académie royale de Belgique, Bulletin de la classe des lettres et des sciences morales et politiques et de la classe des beaux-arts*, ser. 3, 37 (1899): 171–213 at 181–85; Van Meter, "The Peace of Amiens-Corbie," pp. 646–55.

[81] Janssens, "La Paix de Dieu"; Van Meter, "The Peace of Amiens-Corbie," pp. 642–43; Goetz, "Kirchenschutz," pp. 220–21.

[82] *Miracula sancti Adelardi abbatis*, c. 4, *AASS* Jan. I, pp. 118–20 at 119; Van Meter, "The Peace of Amiens-Corbie"; Morelle, "La réécriture de la 'Vita Adalhardi.'"

[83] *Liber miraculorum sancte Fidis*, 1.28, ed. A. Bouillet (Paris, 1897), pp. 71–73.

[84] Mansi, 19:267–68, c. 1.

[85] Mansi, 19:89–90; Gergen, *Pratique juridique*, pp. 51–65.

[86] Good overviews for these councils and the sources for them are provided by Goetz, "Kirchenschutz"; Hoffmann, *Gottesfriede*, chap. 3; Head, "The Development"; Head, "Peace and Power in France Around the Year 1000," *Essays in Medieval Studies* 23 (2006): 1–17.

[87] Magnou-Nortier, "La place du Concile du Puy," pp. 500–03; Mansi, 19:271–72. Note that in Mansi's edition churches are protected save those built in castles; Magnou-Nortier needlessly emends this.

[88] Koziol, "The Conquest of Burgundy"; Riches, "The Peace of God," pp. 207–10; Barthélemy, *L'An mil*, pp. 418–28.

[89] Bonnaud-Delamare, "Les institutions de paix"; Barthélemy, *L'An mil*, pp. 435–39; J.-F. Lemarignier, "Paix et réforme monastique en Flandre et en Normandie autour de l'année 1023. Quelques observations," *Structures politiques et religieuses dans la France du haut Moyen Âge: Recueil d'articles rassamblés par ses disciples* (Rouen: Publications de l'Université de Rouen, 1995), pp. 339–64.

[90] *Miracula sancti Adelardi abbatis*, c. 4, *AASS* Jan. I, p. 119; Van Meter, "The Peace of Amiens-Corbie"; Morelle, "La réécriture de la 'Vita Adalhardi'"; MGH Const. 1, no. 432, p. 616 n. 3.

[91] Van Meter, "The Peace of Amiens-Corbie"; Janssens, "Context of Text?," (above, chap. 1, n. 45); Van Meter, "La Paix de Dieu"; Theo Riches, "Bishop Gerard I of Cambrai-Arras, the Three Orders, and the Problem of Human Weakness," in *The Bishop Reformed: Studies of Episcopal Power and Culture in the Central Middle Ages*, ed. John S. Ott and Anna Trumbore Jones (Aldershot: Ashgate, 2007), pp. 122–36.

[92] Hoffmann, *Gottesfriede*, pp. 144–48; Barthélemy, *L'An mil*, pp. 524–25; MGH Const. 1, no. 422, pp. 599–610, no. 432, p. 616 n. 3.

[93] Vermeesch, *Essai*, pp. 57–66.

[94] Barthélemy, *L'An mil*, p. 523; Hoffmann, *Gottesfriede*, pp. 217–18.

[95] Specific references for most of these instantiations of the Peace will be provided as they are discussed below. Broadly, see the relevant discussions in Barthélemy, *L'An mil*, and Hoffmann, *Gottesfriede*.

[96] *Constitucions*, nos. 1–2, pp. 3–7.

[97] *Constitucions*, no. 3, pp. 8–11.

[98] Mansi, 19:827–32 at c. 3.

[99] Hoffmann, *Gottesfriede*, p. 95; Barthélemy, *L'An mil*, pp. 499–521.

[100] Barthélemy, *L'An mil*, pp. 521–36, 546–50.

[101] Landes, *Relics* (above, n. 73); Michael Frassetto, "Ademar of Chabannes and the Peace of God," in *Where Heaven and Earth Meet: Essays on Medieval Europe in Honor of Daniel F. Callahan*, ed. Michael Frassetto et al. (Leiden: Brill, 2014), pp. 122–37; Anna Trumbore Jones, "Discovering the Aquitainian Church in the Corpus of Ademar of Chabannes," *The Haskins Society Journal* 19 (2007): 82–98; Head, "The Development," pp. 657–58; Head, "Peace and Power," pp. 5–6 (above, n. 86).

[102] Mansi, 19:265–68; *Saint-Maixent*, no. 74, pp. 91–92; *La chronique de Saint-Maixent, 751–1140*, ed. Jean Verdon (Paris: Société d'Édition "Les Belles Lettres," 1979), pp. 106–09.

[103] Head, "The Development," pp. 680–84; Rodulfus Glaber, 4.16, p. 197; Mansi, 19:267: "Constituerunt ut a quinnis praeteritis ..."

[104] CJS, no. 1200.

[105] CJS, no. 1210.

[106] *Saint-Maixent*, no. 93, pp. 113–14.

[107] *Cluny 3*, no. 2255; P.-É. Giraud, *Essai historique sur l'abbaye de S. Barnard et sur la ville de Romans ... Première Partie: Cartulaire de l'église Saint-Barnard de Romans* (Lyon, 1856), no. 11, pp. 28–31.

[108] *Historia patriae monumenta edita iussu regis Caroli Alberti, Chartarum*, vol. 1 (Turin, 1836), cols. 434–36, no. 253 (Newman, no. 57); *RHF* 10:609 (Newman, no. 60). On the council itself, *Miracula sancti Veroli*, *AASS* Jun. III, pp. 384–87 at 385; *Miracula sancti Bercharii*, *RHF* 10:375; *Chronique de Saint-Pierre-le-Vif de Sens, dite de Clarius / Chronicon sancti Petri Vivi Senonensis*, ed. and trans. R.-H. Bautier and Monique Gilles (Paris: Éditions du CNRS, 1979), pp. 114–17.

[109] *Saint-Maixent*, no. 91, pp. 109–11.

[110] Barthélemy, *L'An mil*, pp. 437–68, 547 n. 3, with the literature cited above, n. 91.

[111] Head, "Peace and Power," p. 1 (above, n. 86). Also Head, "The Development," p. 657; Barthélemy, *L'An mil*, p. 261.

[112] Jeffrey A. Bowman, "Councils, Memory and Mills: The Early

Development of the Peace of God in Catalonia," *Early Medieval Europe* 8 (1999): 99–129.

[113] Head, "The Development," pp. 659–66; Bachrach, "Geoffrey Greymantle" (above, chap. 1, n. 53); Bachrach, *Fulk Nerra* (above, chap. 1, n. 53); Jane Martindale, *Status, Authority and Regional Power: Aquitaine and France, 9th to 12th Centuries* (Aldershot: Variorum, 1997), VII and VIII.

[114] Head, "The Development," pp. 666–70; Jones, *Noble Lord*, pp. 97–101; Gergen, *Pratique juridique*, pp. 37–49.

[115] *Saint-Maixent*, no. 74, pp. 91–92.

[116] *Saint-Maixent*, no. 91, pp. 109–11.

[117] Ademar of Chabannes, *Chronicon*, ed. P. Bourgain et al., Corpus Christanorum Continuatio Mediaevalis 129 (Turnhout: Brepols, 1999), 3.56, pp. 175–76, with p. 308 for the date.

[118] Koziol, "The Conquest of Burgundy."

[119] Hoffmann, *Gottesfriede*, pp. 166–68. Barthélemy, *L'An mil*, pp. 524–34, is more doubtful, but the sources and circumstances seem clear enough.

[120] Gergen, *Pratique juridique*. Joachim Gernhuber also argued for the distinctiveness of the Peace of God as legislation, but he embedded his argument in the discredited assumption that legislation was impossible during the early Middle Ages because law was regarded as changeless. Joachim Gernhuber, *Die Landfriedensbewegung in Deutschland bis zum Mainzer Reichslandfrieden von 1235* (Bonn: Ludwig Röhrscheid Verlag, 1952). For the more recent perspective, see Patrick Wormald, *The Making of English Law: King Alfred to the Twelfth Century* (Oxford: Blackwell, 1999).

[121] Above, pp. 20–22.

[122] Codex Vaticanus Reginensis Latinus 1127; Hartmann, "Unbekannte Kanones" (above, chap. 1, n. 40).

[123] MGH Conc. 3, no. 38, pp. 392–94.

[124] MGH Capit. 2, no. 287, pp. 371–75 at 371–72.

[125] Above, pp. 64–65; Mansi, 19:827–32.

[126] Bonnaud-Delamare, "Les institutions de paix," pp. 148–53.

[127] Brown, *Violence* (above, chap. 1, n. 62); Justine Firnhaber-Baker, *Violence and the State in Languedoc, 1250–1400* (Cambridge: Cambridge University Press, 2014). Note the criticisms by Guy Halsall, "Violence and Society in the Early Medieval West: An Introductory Essay," in *Violence and Society in the Early Medieval West*, ed. Guy Halsall (Woodbridge: Boydell, 1998), pp. 1–45.

[128] Koziol, *The Politics of Memory*, pp. 25–26, 40–42, 44 (above, chap. 1, n. 49).

[129] *Cluny* 3, no. 2255 (variant in Mansi, 19:99–102); Barbara Rosenwein, *To Be the Neighbor of Saint Peter: The Social Meaning of Cluny's Property, 909-1049* (Ithaca: Cornell University Press, 1989), pp. 87–88.

[130] Bisson, "The Organized Peace."

[131] *Les miracles de Saint Benoît*, ed. E. de Certain (Paris, 1858), 4.2–4, pp. 192–98; Thomas Head, "The Judgment of God: Andrew of Fleury's Account of the Peace League of Bourges," in *The Peace of God*, ed. Head and Landes, pp. 219–38; Vermeesch, *Essai*, pp. 25–41.

[132] Guy Devailly, *Le Berry du Xᵉ siècle au milieu du XIIIᵉ: Étude politique, religieuse, sociale et économique* (Paris: Mouton, 1973), pp. 146–47 and notes.

[133] Barthélemy, *L'An mil*, pp. 404–13; Devailly, *Le Berry*, pp. 142–48 (above, n. 132).

[134] Gerd Althoff, *Spielregeln der Politik im Mittelalter: Kommunikation in Frieden und Fehde* (Darmstadt: Primus, 1997), pp. 157–84.

[135] Barthélemy, *L'An mil*, pp. 509–10.

[136] Goetz, "Kirchenschutz," pp. 220–21.

[137] *Constitucions*, no. 1, pp. 3–5. Note that extant "letters from heaven" describe the punishments God will inflict on sinners in terms that overlap with formulas of anathema: Delehaye, "Note sur la légende," pp. 177–84 (above, n. 80).

[138] Christian Jaser, *Ecclesia maledicens: Rituelle und zeremonielle Exkommunikationsformen im Mittelalter* (Tübingen: Mohr Siebeck, 2013), pp. 34–45.

[139] *Constitucions*, no. 3, pp. 8–11; Valérie Fortunier and Jacques Pericard, "Odilon et la paix de Dieu," in *Odilon de Mercoeur, L'Auvergne et Cluny: La "Paix de Dieu" et l'Europe de l'an mil* (Nonette: Créer, 2002), pp. 117–34 at 131–33; Mansi, 19:827–32, cc. 26 et al.

[140] Bonnaud-Delamare, "Les institutions de paix"; MGH Const. 1, no. 422, c. 2, p. 600; Bessin, p. 39.

[141] Bessin, p. 39; *Constitucions*, no. 3, pp. 8–11. Among others also Douai, Thérouanne, Arles, Narbonne, and Barcelona, Vic, and Girona.

[142] Daniel Lord Smail, *The Consumption of Justice: Emotions, Publicity, and Legal Culture in Marseille, 1264-1423* (Ithaca: Cornell University Press, 2003).

[143] *Miracula sancti Adelardi*, AASS Jan. I, p. 119.

[144] *Saint-Maixent*, no. 91, pp. 109–11.

[145] Mansi, 19:265–68, c. 1.

[146] Bonnaud-Delamare, "Les institutions de paix," pp. 148–53 (Verdun, Compiègne, Laon, Cambrai); MGH Const. 1, no. 422, pp. 599–601

(Thérouanne); Georges de Manteyer, *Les origines de la Maison de Savoie en Bourgogne, 910-1060*, vol. 3 (1899-1904; reprint Geneva: Mégariotis Reprints, 1978), pp. 91-98 (Vienne).

[147] Paul Fouracre, "Marmoutier and its Serfs in the Eleventh Century," *Transactions of the Royal Historical Society*, ser. 6, 15 (2005): 29-49; Alice Rio, "Freedom and Unfreedom in Early Medieval Francia: The Evidence of the Legal Formulae," *Past and Present* 193 (2006): 7-40.

[148] Ademar, *Chronicon*, 3.35, p. 157 (above, n. 117).

[149] Magnou-Nortier, "La place du Concile du Puy," pp. 500-03.

[150] Mansi, 19:265-68.

[151] *Constitucions*, no. 3, pp. 8-11.

[152] Bonnaud-Delamare, "Les institutions de paix," p. 153; de Manteyer, *Les origines de la Maison de Savoie*, pp. 91-98 (above, n. 146).

[153] *Les miracles de saint Benoît*, ed. de Certain, 5.2, p. 194 (above, n. 131).

Chapter 3

Institutionalizing the Peace and Truce

The majority of books and articles on the Peace and Truce of God are devoted to the period between 989 and ca. 1050—from the first clear appearance of the Peace at Charroux to the time when the articles of the Peace and Truce became fairly standardized. Beyond the mid-eleventh century historians rather lose interest in it. One reason may be a sense that the Peace of God was a failure; for not only did it not bring peace, in some ways it codified the right to violence. A German Peace of 1103 stated this paradox baldly:

> If your enemy meets you on the road, you may harm him if you can. If he flees into anyone's house or homestead, he shall remain unharmed.[154]

If this is what the Peace of God became, it is hard to see it as any kind of turning point in European history. Then, too, the program itself changed, mutating into something recognizably the same yet different. In Bisson's words, it became not just an "instituted" Peace but an "institutionalized" Peace. And increasingly, secular leaders inserted themselves into its proclamation until by the twelfth century one is no longer dealing with a Peace of God at all. It is now the peace of the king, the peace of the prince, the peace of the territory, or the peace of the commune.

The changes did not happen overnight. From the beginning the Peace and Truce had tended to evolve in fits and starts.[155] There was a great surge of Peace activity in the 990s followed by an apparent waning of interest until the development of the Truce in the late 1020s, when a new spate of councils defined the articles of the Peace and Truce more concretely, particularly with respect to enforcement. After the 1050s the movement seemed to ebb again, until a new round of declarations began in the last decade of the eleventh century. Bisson associates this new activity with Urban II's call for a crusade in 1095 at the Council of Clermont, where he promulgated the Truce of God in order to protect the lands of crusaders during their absence.[156] In fact, Norman bishops did establish a Peace and Truce in 1096, spurred on by some of their colleagues who had brought back the decrees of Clermont. Thereafter the Truce of God became a standard fixture of canon law, its basic stipulations repeated at the First, Second, and Third Lateran Councils (1123, 1139, 1179), as well as by Innocent III during his own visit to France in 1130.[157]

But absence of evidence is not evidence of absence. Explicit testimony of Peace councils may have stemmed from moments when the Peace and Truce were being singularly emphasized as an element of policy by political and ecclesiastical leaders. This does not allow us to conclude that the program was otherwise in abeyance. The papal approval of the Truce of God at Clermont did give a boost to the program, as at Rouen in 1096. But when the Peace and Truce were declared at Saint-Omer in 1099, the inspiration was a Peace and Truce established at Soissons in 1093, two years before Clermont.[158] One should therefore not overlook the fact that even during lulls in our documentation we find indications of ongoing Peace activity. For example, Raoul Glaber wrote that the Peace of God was originally meant to be reconfirmed every five years.

Admittedly, we have no good evidence that it was (save a very ambiguous suggestion in the acts of an early Peace of Poitiers), and Raoul himself asserted that the enthusiasm did not last.[159] But in 1033–34 the Peace of Amiens and Corbie required yearly meetings, and this time our source makes it quite clear that such annual meetings really were held. They were still continuing in 1064.[160] The best known Truce of Narbonne was sworn in 1054, but others had been declared there at least once and perhaps twice in the preceding ten years.[161] In Normandy a Peace at Caen, perhaps from 1042–43, was supposed to be confirmed annually for seven years; and though we cannot say with certainty that it was, a Truce was likely established at Caen in both 1047 and 1061–62. Again in Normandy, the Truce was declared at Lisieux in 1064, this council demanding "that the Truce of God be frequently repeated and firmly held." We also know of subsequent declarations of the Truce in Normandy at Lillebonne in 1080 and at Rouen in 1096. As often, there were good, circumstantial political reasons for some of these initiatives: William II's troubled minority had much to do with the first Peace at Caen. The fact remains that there were a good many declarations of the Peace and Truce of God in Normandy.[162] The same was true of Flanders: before the Truce of Saint-Omer in 1099 we hear of a Peace or Truce at Oudenaarde in 1030, at Douai in 1034–35 and probably once later, and at Thérouanne around 1060.[163]

Furthermore, we should not so focus on councils and assemblies that we lose sight of what was happening outside them. The Truce of Caen in 1047 ended with a demand that on Sundays and feast days priests were to bless those who observed the Peace and curse those who violated it.[164] Corbie's "letters from heaven" read as if they were used as templates for sermons on what it meant to observe Sundays, on the necessity of keeping fasts and

vigils and giving alms, and on the dangers to their salvation risked by those who violated the oaths that were
central to the Peace of God.[165] The act of Bishop Oliba of
Vic that first established the Truce of God at Toulouges in
1027 also reads like the outline of a sermon in its explanation of the perils of excommunication. It was very likely
just that. For when Oliba established the Peace and Truce
three years later at Vic, he publicized it in a circular letter
requiring all priests in his diocese to preach the Peace on
Sundays, to excommunicate those who violated it, and to
preach the dangers of such excommunication. Certainly
no one in Oliba's diocese could have avoided knowing
about the Truce, for the bishop also required bells to be
rung in all churches and marketplaces to announce the
beginning of periods of the Truce.[166] In 1060 the monks
of Lobbes toured Flanders with the relics of their patron
saint, preaching peace in all the towns and villages
through which they passed.[167] Even when the Peace was
contested it was still at the centre of public discussions.
On both religious and political grounds, Bishop Gerard I
of Cambrai opposed the Peace of God being promoted in
his diocese by the count of Flanders and the castellan of
Cambrai. Since the two lords used Gerard's stance to por-
tray him as an enemy of peace, the bishop had to preach
at Douai in favour of a Peace that was finally accepted.[168]
When the Truce of God was first proposed in the north
of France it was rejected, at least partly because some
clerics deemed it a "novelty." One wonders whether these
critics shared Gerard of Cambrai's objections to the "total
peace" of Amiens-Corbie: the Truce invited perjury by
encoding standards that were impossible to meet. In any
event, supporters of the program sent Abbot Richard of
Saint-Vanne into the region to preach the Truce. Though
his efforts failed, Richard did preach, as others must have
preached against him, no one espousing war and military

exactions but both sides talking about what peace meant and what the best means were to achieve it.[169]

By the late eleventh and early twelfth century, in France, Germany, and Catalonia, the language of "peace" was everywhere. And not just the language. The articles of the Peace and Truce of God were widely known, fully established, and repeatedly invoked as guidelines for political and military actions. The Peace of God was probably instituted around 1099 for the newly established diocese of Arras. We know it was enforced, for the bishop of Arras, Lambert, threatened to excommunicate the castellan of Lens for violating the lands and atrium of a church if he did not make amends within fifteen days. He actually did excommunicate a provost of the countess of Flanders who had seized the belongings of pilgrims passing through his territory. In each case, Lambert claimed to be applying "the constitution of the Peace" and "the statutes of the Peace."[170] A letter of Ivo of Chartres enjoined all the faithful of his diocese to swear to the "constitution" of the Peace, while his other letters show him enforcing it with excommunications and demanding that other bishops do the same.[171]

The Peace and Truce of God may have ebbed but they did not go away. Though their rules may have been applied inconsistently and opportunistically, they were always part of the arsenal of policies princes and prelates could draw on whenever they needed to reassert their authority. Peace assemblies allowed them to preside over ceremonies that performed their claims to rule in the name of God over the people of God, with a responsibility for peace, justice, and the protection of the unarmed that distinguished their God-given ministries from the mere power of castellans and knights.[172] Yet ceremony was not enough. Neither were decrees of intermittent councils confirmed by mere oaths backed up by the threat of excommunication and eternal damnation. One had to design mechanisms of enforcement. Those mechanisms had to be practicable within existing legal and administrative realities. They could not fly in the face of the values of the military elite whose actions were being regulated and whose cooperation was needed for enforcement. The ways the Peace and Truce of God accomplished all this were their lasting legacies, even if the result was a kind of peace and peace-enforcement that codified violence and had little to do with God, or even the church.

From the Peace of God to the Peace of Valenciennes

The Peace and Truce of God were issued in large councils that usually gathered bishops and other leading figures, both lay and clerical, from multiple ecclesiastical and political jurisdictions. Very quickly—certainly by the time of Verdun-sur-les-Doubs around 1021–22—the articles were "instituted," meaning that the assembly promulgated the articles as a bundle, sometimes called a *forma pacis*. The oaths were then sworn to uphold the Peace (and later the Peace and Truce) as a whole. Bishops attending such councils were supposed to repeat the procedure within their own individual dioceses. The fact that the Peace circulated and was sworn as a package is one reason its articles remained so remarkably stable over the course of the eleventh century. The Truce absolutely prohibited all acts of violence during certain periods of the year: every week from Wednesday at sundown to Monday at sunrise; every year on a substantial number of feast days and their vigils, between the beginning of Advent and the octave of Epiphany, and between Septuagesima Sunday and the octave of Easter or Pentecost. The Peace prohibited actions against certain classes of people, properties, and places: clerics, monks, nuns, women, pilgrims, and those travelling with them without arms; unarmed merchants going to and from markets; the animals necessary to peasants (such as cattle, asses, sheep, goats, and pigs); churches, their immediate surroundings, buildings within their circuits, and cemeteries. The sanctions of the Peace were also quite stable. Excommunication remained the primary sanction for any violation of the Peace, and its purpose also remained the same: to put social pressure on violators of the Peace in order to bring them to reconciliation. Being within or without the Peace was itself used as a sanction, since its usual protections ceased to apply to places and people deemed outside of it, making exclusion from the Peace a kind of outlawry. For example, in the Peaces of Soissons and Saint-Omer (1093, 1099) churches and their atria were under the protection of the Peace unless a fortification within their circuits was being used as a base for looting and storing plunder. In that case, the victims were to make a formal complaint (*clamor*) to the bishop or his archdeacon. If justice were not done within fifteen days, the church and its atrium would be placed "outside our peace" (*extra pacem nostram*).[173] As in earlier Peaces, classes of persons normally protected by the Peace became subject to vengeance (*vindicetur*) if they violated it. Also as before, the Peace and Truce were not intended to replace ordinary legal procedures (whether ecclesiastical or secular) but to supplement them. Almost all Peaces of the second half of the eleventh century not only imposed penance on those who committed homicide in violation of the Peace but also exiled the killer.[174] Catalan Peaces added that in order to receive absolution the killer first had to make a composition for the homicide (that is, make an agreement with the victim's family for compensation).[175] Far from Catalonia, the Peace of Thérouanne applied roughly the same rule to all serious violations of the Peace: thirty years of penance performed in exile, and before departing the guilty "will amend whatever he did against the peace."[176] Southern Peaces consistently required violators to make amends within fifteen days of a complaint, otherwise they were to pay double composition.[177] A similar rule applied in some northern Peaces: after a formal warning, violators of the Peace were to compensate the victim for the loss, pay a fine of nine pounds for the infraction, and "do justice according to the law of the country."[178] The law of the country also applied to those who denied having committed the infraction of which they stood accused or who denied having violated it "knowingly": they were to purge themselves on oath. That is, they and twelve of their "peers" were to swear a formal oath stating their innocence. Interestingly, the rule applied not only to "nobles and knights" but also to "villeins," the only difference being that a villein's lord had to swear as well.[179]

As with the early program so with the later: there was no inconsistency, let alone any contradiction, between the Peace and Truce of God and secular notions and practices of justice. Quite the contrary, the Peace and Truce relied on compurgation with oathhelpers, the payment of fines to lords, the payment of compensation to victims, and exile. Excommunication or its threat simply provided an additional goad by making ordinary social interaction difficult for someone who had violated the rules. In what fundamental ways, then, did the Peace and Truce of the late eleventh and early twelfth centuries differ from what they had been? The specifics of an answer differ according to region, but the two basic trends were largely the same everywhere in the former West Frankish kingdom (including the south of the old Spanish march, that is, Catalonia). First, the Peace and Truce were institutionalized locally through the creation of permanent procedures, offices, and revenues that made enforcement of the Peace no longer dependent on periodic declarations of assemblies. Second, secular princes increasingly took over elements of the Peace of God and made them the core of their own developing legislative experiments.

One should begin in northern France, because historians have traditionally associated these changes in the Peace with the creation of strong principalities; and the epitomes of strong territorial princes were the counts or margraves of Flanders and the dukes of Normandy. Both rulers benefitted from the wealth generated by cities that had already become centres of trade or industry. Both controlled coherent territories in which other lords were clearly subordinate. Both were developing administrations in which appointed agents represented the rulers' interests locally in matters both fiscal and judicial. Neither ruler was challenged by the church. The Norman episcopacy was largely supportive of ducal authority, the ecclesiastical province of Rouen being coterminous with the duchy. In Flanders episcopal power was fairly weak, primarily because diocesan capitals were located on the margins of the principality; as a result, no bishops commanded significant political power or economic resources in the core of the counts' territories. Finally, even though the king of France exercised no direct power over the two principalities, posed no danger to their rulers, and sometimes was in bitter conflict with them, the idea of kingship was still a presence—a model of political authority to be imitated. In fact, both Flanders and Normandy were frequently referred to as "kingdoms" (*monarchiae*, *regna*). Though that did not make their rulers kings, it did make their positions within their territories notably king-like.[180]

These conditions shaped the reception of the Peace of God in the north of the kingdom, one element in particular. It had already appeared in the Peace of Verdun-sur-le-Doubs established by Robert the Pious's agents following his takeover of the duchy of Burgundy in 1016. As usual, this Peace prohibited certain military actions by the oathswearer, but it allowed an important exemption: when he was participating in military campaigns and sieges of castles as part of the army of the archbishop of Lyon, the local diocesan bishop, the count, or the king. A similar reserve was repeated in the oath that Bishop Warin of Beauvais had approved by Robert the Pious himself in 1023: the swearer promised to respect the Peace towards those who swore it and kept it, save for those lands under his own lordship, and save for the building and besieging of castles when serving "in the army of the king or our bishops." Such reserves appeared in all subsequent issues of the Peace and Truce from northern France that stemmed from Verdun and Compiègne: Laon, Douai, Thérouanne, and Caen. The most significant differences were that in Flanders the reserve favoured the count rather than the king, in Normandy both the count and the king.[181] The reserves did not mean that armies of the count and king were exempt from the Peace and Truce, allowed to commit any actions they wished. Even when serving in the army of king, count, or bishop, a participant in the Peace was still restricted in the requisitions he could take in support of his military service. For example, he could require no more than was necessary for food (Caen), or for feeding horses (Thérouanne), or for supplies (Verdun and Compiègne). Verdun further stipulated that the oathswearer would not violate the protected areas of churches (*salvamenta*) unless he had been denied supplies he was owed or the right to buy supplies beyond what he was owed. The variations did not affect the essential principle: throughout northern France, the Peace affirmed that military campaigns of kings, counts, and bishops were different from *werrae*. The exception comes through most clearly in an addendum to the Peace of Saint-Omer in 1099, which specifically stated that the count of Flanders, Robert II, agreed to apply the Peace "throughout his land," with three reserves: if he went on military expeditions with the king, or on military expeditions against the count of Hainaut (at the time his enemy), or if a castle in his "kingdom" was handed over to an enemy or built without his permission. In this last case, the count "shall take and destroy it by arms whether in peace or in war."[182]

If one takes these reserves literally, they would mean that any military action by a king or a count was by definition not a *werra* but a legitimate military action, a kind of "just war" no matter what its cause. As Bisson remarked, this is why the great princes did not regard the Peace and Truce as posing any danger to them: the *forma pacis* explicitly recognized their authority and safeguarded their means of imposing it militarily.[183] Even more important, it allowed them to take control of the Peace by making it an expression of their own authority and allowing them to justify their military campaigns as campaigns to enforce the Peace. How early this began we cannot say precisely. It is likely that as at Poitiers, early Norman and Flemish Peaces were staged to underscore the cooperative authority of both the prince and the bishops, who acted alongside and in support of each other; at least, this is how the actions are represented in the sources. Unfortunately, those sources are late and not fully reliable.[184] Yet there is no doubt that by the end of the eleventh century the dukes of Normandy and counts of Flanders had taken a more active role in representing themselves as sponsors of Peaces. The Peace of Lillebonne of 1080, whose canons we have in a fairly trustworthy transmission, begins, "The Peace of God, called in the vernacular the Truce, shall be steadfastly observed as it was when it was first established by Prince William himself."[185] In Flanders, Count Robert the Frisian agreed to the Peace established by bishops at Saint-Omer in 1099.[186] But just before he died in 1111, he promulgated a peace on his own. As soon as he succeeded his father, Baldwin VII had this peace renewed. Baldwin issued further peace declarations in 1114 and around 1120, as did, evidently, his successor Charles the Good near the beginning of his reign.[187]

While overlapping with and building on the Peace and Truce of God, these princely peaces appear to have been significantly different from them. It is as if the princes had separated out those elements of the Peace and Truce most relevant to them, not repudiating the Peace and Truce but creating a prince's peace that coordinated with them, just as the Peace and Truce had coordinated with secular legal practices. Thus, according to a nearly contemporary description by a canon of Saint-Omer, the peace of Robert the Frisian in 1111 was quite simple:

> Peace. A noble and a knight shall purge themselves by the oath of twelve of their peers. A villein and anyone else [shall swear] with the same number of their equals, with his lord swearing at the same time, and saving the rights of justice and customs of our church. This peace Robert will preserve throughout his entire land as will his men towards each other for the love of God, such that, however, if a castle was betrayed in his kingdom or built without his permission, whether in peace or in war, he might take it or destroy it with arms, and he might also make [military] campaigns with the king and his own campaigns against the land of his cousin B[aldwin, count of Hainaut].[188]

This peace of 1111 was largely an abbreviation of the Peace of Saint-Omer. A peace declared by Robert's son Baldwin VII was somewhat different, although it is hard to interpret because our source for it is so late. It prohibited nighttime attacks on persons and dwellings, and all acts or even threats of arson, on penalty of death. No one was allowed to bear arms save the bailiffs of the count, the guardians of his strongholds (*arcium*), and his other officials. Homicides and woundings were to be punished by the *lex talionis*, unless the accused could prove self-defence by a judicial duel or an ordeal. For all other crimes one could make compensation, but the count's bailiff or other agent would receive double the amount as a fine.[189] This was obviously not the Peace of God. Its penalties—for that matter its entire perspective on crime and punishment—were however, very close to those we find in the contemporary German "territorial peace" (*Landfriede*).

Despite its brevity and obscure transmission, this peace does contain important clues about its purposes. The prohibitions against bearing arms make little sense for the military aristocracy but a great deal of sense within towns. *Arces* were not castles in the countryside but usually fortified towers in castles built within the walls of towns. Flemish bailiffs were comital officials stationed in towns with comital castles. Arson was a particular problem in towns. Finally, "they called this peace a commune and a truce" (*communem … herilemque*) to be sworn on oath in the territory of Ypres by both "the leading men and the people" (*procerumque et populi*).[190] All these hints suggest that this "peace" was actually the establishment of something like a commune at Ypres, sworn to not just by the *populi* of Ypres and its vicinity but also by the *proceres*, because the latter would have to respect the laws being granted. In fact, such "communes" become visible at just this moment in the Low Countries, and an early term for them was "peace" (*pax*). The best known is the "peace of Valenciennes," established by the count of Hainaut in 1114, but there were many others that slowly come into view, Cambrai, Saint-Amand, and Tournai among them.[191] The laws that first governed them are hard to get at, since they, too, are usually transmitted only in later sources. Even that of Valenciennes is extant not in its original form but in a much later text. But the core elements, principles, and language are clear enough from the Valenciennes charter. There was a sworn "peace," its participants called "men of the peace" (*viri pacis*). The burghers who swore the peace were allowed to name "lords of the peace" (*domini pacis*) who governed it. Merchants travelling to and from Valenciennes were protected from seizures of their persons and property. Specific violations of the peace were spelled out. Those accused of violations of the peace could be held guilty if convicted by the testimony of two "men of the peace." If such testimony could not be produced the accused could clear himself by duel or by oaths. Depending on the seriousness of the offence, those found guilty of violating the peace suffered penalties ranging from hanging to mutilation to the payment of amends and fines divided between the victim and the count.[192]

Like Baldwin VII's Flemish peace, the peace of Valenciennes was not a Peace of God: bishops were entirely absent from its promulgation; it spelled out details of secular procedures; it punished infractions with secular, not ecclesiastical, sanctions. Yet its terms would have been inconceivable without the Peace of God. There were those within the peace and those outside it. Membership in the peace was established by an oath, and the oath was mandatory. One did not "commit a crime"; rather, one "violated the peace" (*infrangere pacem*), exactly the same phrase used for violations of the Peace of God. The peace included both elites and non-elites and was equally binding on both. The military elites bound themselves on oath not to seize persons and properties of non-elites. Infractions of the peace were usually settled by composition between the parties, payment of damages, and a fine, and every effort was taken to ensure that disputes were brought before judicial tribunals before parties resorted to self-help.

It is noteworthy that the language of peace was pronounced and durable in Flanders but much less so in Normandy after the Peace at Lillebonne in 1080. The reason cannot be that the duke of Normandy was so powerful that he was able to create a judicial administration that centred on him and his officials. The counts of Flanders were equally powerful. They, too, were developing an administrative system staffed by appointed officials. And although Flanders passed through moments of tremendous strife, that was no less true of Normandy, and during those crises the dukes of Normandy took full advantage of episcopal support and welcomed episcopal councils that vaunted the dukes as the protectors of the poor and defenceless.[193] Yet in Normandy the Peace of God receded in frequency and prominence, and the "peace of the duke" never developed into a principle of law and order as it did in Flanders. One reason may be that Flanders remained influenced by the *Landfrieden* of neighbouring German territories. Another possibility is that the Norman dukes never promoted communes as semi-autonomous islands of local associative organization. The counts of Flanders did. The communes of Flanders acted as a kind of reservoir of peace language and peace-making practices that kept the discourse of peace alive in Flanders and made it an important part of political staging and rulership. And just as in the Peace of God, so communal peace and the "peace of the count" provided frameworks for continuing legislative amendation and innovation, which is why it is so difficult to uncover the "original" terms of the peace of Valenciennes: it kept being added to and amended.

Louis VI's Diocesan Militias

Early Flemish communes resulted from a bargain between townsmen and the counts. In return for limited rights of self-government, the towns collectively fulfilled certain obligations to the counts, including the duty of providing militias to serve in their host. These militias are well documented, because they fought often and well during the terrible civil war that wracked Flanders after the assassination of Charles the Good in 1127.[194] But communes were not unique to Flanders. They are documented for a number of towns in northern France: Cambrai (1077), Saint-Quentin (ca. 1081), Beauvais (ca. 1099), Noyon (1108–09), Mantes (1110), Laon (ca. 1109–12), Amiens (ca. 1113), Corbie (1123), Saint-Riquier (1126), and Soissons (1116–26).[195] There were doubtless others. The example of Le Mans is particularly well-known, and particularly instructive. After the count of Maine died without a male heir in 1062, William of Normandy took control of the region, setting up castles and installing his own garrisons. When William left the continent to conquer England, "the leading men of Maine, together with the people, defected from his fidelity as one." Eventually a local magnate, Geoffrey of Mayenne, took over the leadership of the rebels, but he made himself unpopular with the "citizens" (*cives*) by demanding new exactions (*exactionibus*). In response, the "citizens" made a sworn association:

> Making a conspiracy, which they called a commune, all bound themselves equally by oaths and forced Geoffrey and other leading men of the region to bind themselves by oaths to their conspiracy against their wills.

The commune enforced the oath with sanctions that included hanging and blinding, in other words, not just amends but corporal punishments—a phenomenon we also find in the peaces of Flanders, Hainaut, and Germany. It also raised a military force combining the retinues of the *proceres* and its own militia, and began to attack and destroy the castles of their enemies (*adversarii*), who were less enemies of Geoffrey of Mayenne or William of Normandy than enemies of their own peace association. For that is what this early commune of Le Mans was, as its army marched against castles behind the crosses and banners of churches carried by priests and led by the bishop of Le Mans himself. Its laws were called "holy institutions" (*sanctis instructionibus*). The militia even attacked castles during Lent, a period of the Truce. Our hostile source calls attention to this as evidence of the participants' impiety; in fact, nowhere did the Truce ever apply to "rebels" against the Peace.[196]

In studying the commune of Le Mans and its militia, one cannot help being reminded of the Peace militia established by Archbishop Aimo of Bourges around 1038, for it, too, marched on castles behind banners of saints carried by priests. The most important difference appears to have been that Aimo instituted the Peace and organized "the people of Bourges" into a militia; the people of Le Mans organized a militia themselves and dragooned the bishop into leading it. However, other bishops in France did organize militias on the model of Bourges, for they are explicitly mentioned in a number of Peace statutes. Unusually, the Peace of Rouen in 1096 records the words of the oath that was actually sworn. The largest part of the oath concerns the swearer's military obligations:

> Hear this, that from this day forward I will faithfully keep this establishment of the Truce of God as here set forth, and I will bring my aid to my bishop or archdeacon against all who will have refused to swear this establishment or do not observe it, such that if he summons me to move against them I will neither evade nor neglect the summons but with my arms I will march with him and give help against them so far as I am able, by my faith, without subterfuge, according to my conscience. So help me God and these saints.[197]

In the same decade the Peaces of Soissons and Saint-Omer made very similar requirements: if the bishop, upon the counsel of good men, decided to "lead the army" against anyone who had been excommunicated for having refused to swear the Peace or for having violated its terms, then all the bishop's parishioners were to "aid him in defending the peace together (*communiter*)."[198] In Burgundy, also in 1099, the bishop-elect of Autun led "the sworn commune of the dioceses of Autun and Chalon" against Flavigny, whose abbot and people had rejected his fiscal demands and judicial claims.[199]

These sworn militias came not only from the bishop's own city. As at Bourges in 1038, the Peace and Truce of God were binding on all members of a diocese, its oaths sworn not just in the episcopal sees but in localities as well. The obligation to serve in a militia to enforce the Peace was therefore incumbent on all adult males in a diocese. The requirement was not a mere formality. It was applied. In fact, it was relied on by the king of France himself, Louis VI.

The domains of the early Capetians varied greatly in the density of the kings' rights and revenues. Their resources were largely concentrated in and around Senlis, Paris, and Orléans. Along the lower Loire between Blois and the coast they really had no material resources and little way to enforce their will save by negotiation, alliance, and warfare. North and east of Senlis they had important but highly scattered resources.[200] Mostly they relied on the loyalty of key *fideles* and shifting, opportunistic alliances with the greater northern princes. Above all, they relied on abbots and bishops. The prelates gave the king much more than moral support. They provided him with troops, some from their own vassalic retinues, but some composed of the local militias of cities, towns, and their environs. The testimony of the Norman chronicler Orderic Vitalis is explicit on this score. For example, Orderic described a two-month siege of the castle of Bréval in 1094 by King Philip I and Duke Robert Curthose. The besieging force included parishioners led by priests bearing the banners of their churches.[201] Orderic also wrote that in his early campaigns against the castellans of the royal domain, Louis VI sought aid of his bishops. "Therefore the bishops established a popular commune in France, so that priests would accompany the king in battles and sieges with their banners and all their parishioners."[202] Again according to Orderic, following a serious defeat in Normandy at Brémule in 1119, Louis was advised to gather an army of bishops, counts, and other lords, and also "priests with all their parishioners," so that "a common army can exact common vengeance on enemies." Accordingly, on Louis's instructions the bishops commanded the priests of their dioceses to gather their parishioners and follow the king in his expedition against "the Norman rebels."[203] That these parochial armies were, in fact, Peace militias is shown first by the fact that they were summoned on the authority of bishops under threat of excommunication, and second by a detail about the siege of Bréval: it occurred during Lent, which would ordinarily have been a violation of the Truce, except that the fortification had been built within the circuit of a monastery, which meant that it was no longer protected by the Truce.

To say that Louis VI needed the Peace and Truce because he was a weak king is true enough, but it also misrepresents the situation. Louis VI was "weak" because the kingdom's unwritten constitution allowed counts, viscounts, and other lords so much political and jurisdictional autonomy. As we have seen, the Peace of God actually sanctioned this political structure by allowing lords great freedom of action within their own districts and by permitting them to use military action when asserting legal claims as long as they respected the limitations imposed by the *forma pacis*. Furthermore, in eleventh- and early twelfth-century France jurisdictions were a tangled network of overlapping and competing rights of lordship: within any ten-mile area, even within any given village

or estate, a number of lords had some sort of justice—
bishops, monasteries, counts, viscounts, *vicedomini*, castellans, advocates, *vicarii*, provosts, and even communes.
Friction and conflict over rights were inevitable. Perhaps
most important of all, in those military actions in which
he employed Peace militias, Louis was acting in regions
in which his own rights of lordship were least secure both
politically and legally. What gave him the right to inter-
vene at Bréval? What gave him the right to fight against
Enguerrand of Coucy, Thomas of Marle, Theobald of Blois,
or Henry I of Normandy? The Peace of God gave Louis
political cover for the assertion of his authority by placing his actions under its sanction. And Louis used it. At
some point before 1114 he himself instituted a peace.
It may have been in 1111, as a prelude to his first campaign against Hugh of Le Puiset, when at Melun a gathering of archbishops, bishops, clerics, and monks asked
the king for military aid against Hugh, whom the prelates
condemned in the language of Peace councils as "a most
rapacious plunderer" (*rapacissimum predonem*).[204] Louis
certainly benefitted from a redeclaration of the Peace in
1107 by the pope himself at a council in Troyes.[205] One sus-
pects that Louis purposely mobilized the Peace to justify
his campaigns against Thomas of Marle in the Amiénois
and Laonnois. For immediately before the king undertook
any military action, two ecclesiastical councils met within a
month of each other in late 1114 and early 1115 under the
authority of a papal legate and excommunicated Thomas
for acts of rapine and plunder against churches and the
poor. Only then did Louis march. After two years of campaigning Louis finally took Thomas's castles. Fighting in
his army was Count William II of Nevers, who was captured
and imprisoned on the orders of Count Theobald of Blois.
At Louis's personal request the papal legate excommunicated those who had ambushed William and threatened

Theobald with excommunication if he did not free him. In response, Theobald professed astonishment that the king would have had him condemned by ecclesiastical judges rather than summoned before a royal court. Nevertheless, Theobald stated his willingness to appear before "judges of the peace" and there prove that his knights had done nothing "against the pact of peace." However, Theobald was being disingenuous and Louis was being canny. The campaigns against Thomas of Marle had been justified in terms of the Peace of God. The Peace granted safe conducts to all those going to or returning from military expeditions against those excommunicated as violators of the Peace. Theobald had unmistakably violated the Peace and was subject to its jurisdiction.[206]

The Peace in Germany

As the above examples demonstrate, the Peace and Truce of God did not disappear after the 1070s; but they were evolving rapidly and diverging regionally, as princes and prelates adapted the program to the political structures and capacities of their own territories. Nowhere were such adaptations more pronounced than in lands ruled by the kings of Germany.[207] Here something like the Peace and Truce of God first appeared at Liège in 1082, then the next year at Cologne. One should note the participants and the timing. In these years Henry IV, not yet emperor, was embattled in Italy and again under excommunication. The bishops of Liège and Cologne were two of his staunchest supporters in the German church. In a letter announcing his Peace, the archbishop of Cologne wrote that he had acted because violence was tearing apart his diocese. Historians regard his explanation sceptically, as deployments of standard Peace rhetoric, since there is no evidence of any surge of violence at the time and no reason there should have been—in marked contrast to a decade earlier, when dissension and violence at Cologne had been quite real. It is more likely that the two bishops' declaration of the Peace was a strong performative statement that they and the people and princes of their dioceses stood united with the king against his enemies.[208] But the king's enemies could play the same game. In 1084 at Goslar in Saxony (the heartland of resistance to Henry), bishops and princes opposed to the king swore their own Peace, in direct response to the Peace of Cologne. Henry's riposte came the next year at Mainz where just after Easter, in the company of his own antipope, he gathered his supporters and "by common consent and counsel the Peace of God was established." In 1103, having reconciled with the Saxons, Henry held another assembly at Mainz, this time during the week of Epiphany, where he announced his plans to go to the Holy Land and issued a Peace to last four years. Late in 1104 Henry V rebelled against his father. In 1105, having gained the support of Bavarian, Swabian, and Franconian princes, he went to Quedlinburg and Nordhausen, the leading memorial centres of the old Saxon dynasty. In the assembly at Nordhausen, on the day after Pentecost he publicly pledged his support to the reform program of the Roman papacy and "confirmed the Peace of God."[209] The pattern continued throughout the twelfth and thirteenth centuries. Almost every German ruler issued a Peace, usually in major assemblies that marked some crucial political moment: thus Frederick Barbarossa in 1152 around the time of his coronation, in 1158 at the famous Diet of Roncaglia, and in 1179, when he was laying the groundwork for the trial of Duke Henry the Lion.[210] Henry VII's defiance of his father Frederick II was signalled by his declaration of a Peace in 1234. The next year Frederick came to Germany, tried and imprisoned his son, and issued his own Peace in its place.[211]

German historians call these Peaces declared by kings or emperors *Reichsfrieden*, because they were normally issued for the entire kingdom by its ruler. For a long time they were given a privileged place in German constitutional history as stages by which German rulers slowly wrested political and judicial power from the church and asserted a claim to something like judicial suzerainty over the kingdom. In fact, contemporaries themselves treated these royal Peaces as privileged, as shown by the fact that the greatest of all German legal customaries, the *Sachsenspiegel*, begins with Frederick II's 1235 *Reichsfriede*, as if the emperor's authority validated all the rules that followed.[212] In contrast, recent historians have questioned the practical effect of the *Reichsfrieden*, for two reasons especially. First, German kings never had the administrative capacity to enforce the decrees. This left disputes to be settled regionally and locally according to established rules and procedures. Second, the *Reichsfrieden* themselves incorporated rules and procedures already established regionally; and the regional framework within which such rules and procedures had developed was a distinct kind of Peace, the *Landfriede*, which ultimately descended from the Peaces of Liège and Cologne, and which derived legitimacy not from any royal approval or even initiative but instead from agreements of regional leaders acting cooperatively and swearing a *forma pacis* on oath.

Historians no longer doubt, as they once did, that the Peaces of Liège and Cologne were offshoots of the Peace of God, probably inspired by examples in nearby Flanders. Cologne offers the better example because the archbishop himself recorded its terms in the letter mentioned above. He states that the "decree of peace" established periods of truce for the coming year; the times specified are largely those covered by the Truce of God in France. During these periods there was to be no killing, arson, or pillaging, nor assaults of any sort made with any kind of weapon, including simple clubs. From Advent to the week after Epiphany and from Septuagesima Sunday to the week after Pentecost, no one was to carry arms at all. As in contemporary northern French models, military expeditions ordered by the king were exempted from the Truce, and public officials (dukes, counts, advocates, and their agents) were at all times allowed to enforce court judgements against violators of the Peace. The right of asylum in churches and cemeteries was explicitly confirmed. Those who did not observe the terms of the Peace were to be excommunicated, denied even the viaticum if dying.

Nevertheless, the *Landfriede* was not quite the same thing as the Peace of God. In the first place, at Cologne and apparently also at Liège, no special protection was given to unarmed clerics, monks, women, and merchants. This omission was corrected in a few subsequent *Landfrieden* and *Reichsfrieden*, such as Mainz in 1085 and 1103 and Bavaria in 1094. The Rhineland Peace of 1179, established under the auspices of Frederick Barbarossa, explicitly protected not only clerics, monks, women, and merchants, but also farmers (*agricolae*), millers, hunters (but not poachers), Jews pertaining to the imperial fisc, and all inhabitants of towns and villages. Still, the fact that only a minority of German Peaces singled out specific categories of persons for protection while the majority did not suggests that their frequent omission was intentional and significant. In effect, *Landfrieden* subjected everyone within a given territory to the same prohibitions regardless of legal status, though somewhat different rules of proof and punishment applied to the unfree.

Such social inclusiveness was probably a by-product of other differences between the *Landfrieden* and French Peaces. In France, the Peace was originally issued in councils of bishops who were to implement the Peace within

their own dioceses. This remained true even in Normandy
and Flanders towards the end of the eleventh century. To
be sure, these bishops were also powerful temporal lords,
and in articulating the Peace they acted with members
of the lay aristocracy. Yet its ambit remained defined in
terms of dioceses. When the counts of Flanders began
issuing Peaces, they were defined as applying throughout
"his entire land" or "principality," and were very much an
expression of a claim to dominance over the subaltern
lords of their territory. As for Germany, the Peaces of Liège
and Cologne were established under the aegis of the cities' bishops and so ran throughout their dioceses; but the
area covered by *Landfrieden* soon came to be defined very
differently. A contemporary chronicler described a Peace
declared at Ulm in 1094 as first being introduced to Bavaria
and later to Franconia and Alsace.[213] Frederick Barbarossa's Rhineland Peace of 1179 delimited the area within
which it would apply in terms of named rivers, bridges,
roads, and the boundaries and junctures of dioceses and
counties. In other words, as the name suggests, the territory covered by a *Landfriede* was not defined in terms
of ecclesiastical jurisdictions. And this difference must be
bound up with another. The 1094 Bavarian Peace was initiated not by bishops but by the duke of Bavaria, acting
in consort with the duke of Swabia "and other Alamannic
princes." A 1094 Peace attributes its institution to "the
Alsatians, along with their *primates*," a term that may refer
to bishops but more likely means magnates. The 1200
Landfriede of Hainaut was the work of the count of Hainaut
and "his noble men and other knights." Even the Peace
of Valais (1179–89), sworn under the aegis of the bishop
of Sion and written down by his chaplain, was enacted in
his capacity as count of the Valais, not bishop of Sion.[214]

The fact that lay magnates (and bishops acting in their
capacity as temporal rather than spiritual lords) coordi-

nated these German Peaces surely explains what has always been regarded as their most distinctive character-istic, especially since the Peaces issued in the name of the counts of Flanders shared the same trait. They went into great detail about the specifics of worldly crimes and torts and the corporal punishment of such acts. For example, the Bavarian Peace of 1094 distinguished between thefts of goods valued at one *solidus* and five *solidi*, punishing the former with beating and a two-fold amendation, the latter with blinding or amputation of a hand or foot. The Swa-bian Peace of 1104 punished a thief who stole goods worth less than five *solidi* by beating him, shaving his head, and branding his jaw. The Rhineland Peace of 1179 punished homicide with capital punishment, woundings with loss of a hand. In many Peaces one finds sentences of banish-ment rather than excommunication. Many punished those who aided or harboured violators of the Peace with the same punishments the violators themselves would suffer. For violations committed by knights, the Peace of Hainaut says tersely, "Death for death, member for member."

Of course, one cannot take these Peaces as providing a full picture of the workings of German dispute-resolution. Just as the Peace of God stipulated ecclesiastical sanctions, leaving secular procedures and punishments unstated but implied, so German Peaces may have stipulated secular procedures and punishments, not stating but permitting a panoply of ecclesiastical ones. Certainly *Landfrieden* and *Reichsfrieden* left room for negotiated settlements; a few charters even show the possibility of corporal punish-ment compelling parties to seek peaceful resolutions.[215] German Peaces also paid a great deal of attention to the procedures by which individuals could clear themselves of accusations, usually by compurgation, a mode of proof that was as much a test of an accused person's reputation as his guilt or innocence. Restored to their full social context, the actual workings of German and French Peaces may not have differed all that much. Nevertheless, the *forma pacis* that was sworn differed greatly.

The distinctiveness of the German *formae pacis* returns us to what continued to be the most important aspect of the Peace of God and its derivatives: the *forma pacis* remained a superb framework for making and codifying law. For that is what the *Landfrieden* and *Reichsfrieden* were: written records of legal rules recognized, created, modified, and accepted on oath by lords of a territory acting together. For example, the 1084 Peace of Goslar stated that a traveller might take at most three handfuls of hay from a field to feed their horses. A decade later, the Peace of Alsace allowed a traveller to take only what was necessary for the horse he was riding, and then only while on a public road. The Rhineland Peace of 1179 was more specific still: a traveller needing to feed his horse had to keep one foot on the road, and using a knife or sickle cut only as much grass as he could reach and only as much as he needed at that moment, taking nothing with him. Anyone who left the road and entered a field to cut grass or who took grass away with him would be hanged as a thief. There are many such rules in the German Peaces about many different issues: selling goods to travellers; the hue and cry and fines and punishments for not heeding it; the number and length of periods of truce required before an individual could be deemed outside the Peace; insults; poaching; the different punishments meted out to thieves caught red-handed a first time versus a second time; the obligation to report a lost horse; the locations where one could and could not burn charcoal; the kinds of knives prohibited from being carried; the number of supporters one might bring to court and the weapons they were permitted to carry.[216] It is not too much to say that the *Landfrieden* created German law. Without them, the *Sachsenspiegel* would never have been possible.

The Institutionalized Peace in the South

The Truce of God first appeared in Catalonia in 1030 and 1033 under Bishop Oliba of Vic. An incidental statement in the 1033 acts reveals that the Peace and Truce were also being declared in another core Catalan diocese, Girona. The same acts indicate the active presence of "counts, viscounts and other magnates and God-fearing Christians," while one clause required fines for violations of the peace to be divided between the bishop and the count. As often in this period, the Peace and Truce were being declared with the cooperation of local secular leaders, not against them.[217] Then an assembly at Barcelona in 1064 marked the same sort of change we see in Normandy and Flanders: the more active participation of a prince using the assembly to show himself in a position of leadership. For this Peace was confirmed by the bishops of the leading sees of Catalonia acting together (Barcelona, Vic, and Girona), along with abbots and clerics, "at the order of Lord Raimund and Lady Almodis, princes of Barcelona, with the assent and acclamation of their magnates of the land and other God-fearing Christians."[218] Between 1064 and 1066 the Peace and Truce were declared again for Vic, Girona, and Barcelona. The act states that its articles also applied to Empúries, Peralada, and Roussillon. In fact, during these very same years a separate constitution of the Peace was issued in an assembly at Toulouges (in the diocese of Elne) under the presidency of the archbishop of Narbonne (the metropolitan) but on the obvious initiative of the bishops of Girona and Elne. This Peace specifically noted the presence and agreement of the counts of Besalú, Cerdanya, Roussillon, and Empúries (who ruled Peralada).[219] One of the major purposes of this set of Peaces in 1064–66 was to prepare a proto-crusade against Barbastro by placing the lands of all participants in the campaign under the protection of the Truce of God—this thirty years before Urban II did the same at Clermont. But it also accomplished something else: by extending the same Peace and Truce to counties that were within the count of Barcelona's sphere of influence but not yet his, it reinforced Barcelona's hegemony and paved the way for the counts' takeover of the other Pyrenaean counties a few decades later.

Over the course of the next century, the counts of Barcelona neatly appropriated the Peace and Truce of God for themselves. In 1108 Ramón Berenguer III borrowed the protections of the Peace and Truce to attract settlers to help rebuild and secure the castellany of Olèrdola. This time the protections were issued in the name of the count himself, the bishop of Barcelona being mentioned as merely advising.[220] When the same count took over the counties of Cerdanya and Conflent in 1118, he established a peace in the counties protecting oxen and other plow animals and those who worked with them. Although he issued the charter granting this peace alongside the bishop of Elne, still it was Ramón Berenguer's role that was privileged, both by his title ("by the grace of God count of Barcelona and marquis of Provence") and by the fact that fines for violating the peace were to be paid in his coinage.[221] The culmination of this shift came in 1164 when the count of Barcelona, now also king of Aragon, issued a formal charter at his Aragonese capital of Zaragoza two years after the beginning of his reign. According to its text, he himself had ordered the convening of the assembly, whose members included bishops, the masters of the Knights Templar, the barons of Aragon, and representatives of the major cities of the realm. He had summoned it on account of "the many violations of *my* peace." As part of his peace, he stated that anyone who refused to hand over castles when required would lose their lands. And anyone who "violated my truces and the truces of Christians or Saracens" and who committed seizures on the king's highways (*depredaverit*) or acts of plundering on the king's lands (*predam vel ropariam fecerit*) was to amend within twenty days of a warning or lose his honour and lands because guilty of treason (*regie magestatis reus*). The Peace of God had become the peace of a king. But the basic terms were much the same. Also the same was that this peace still required an oath: Alfonso II's constitution was sworn individually by forty-four named officials and magnates.[222]

Given its trajectory in Normandy, Flanders, Germany, and Catalonia, one might think that the history of the Peace of God conforms to a very traditional grand narrative of a shift from a sacramental peace organized by the church (in particular bishops) to a secular peace serving the interests of rulers, but one should not exaggerate the difference. Despite a handful of strongly ideological statements like Frederick II's *Constitutions of Melfi* and Marsilius of Padua's *Defensor pacis*, in reality law and political power in the later Middle Ages never became purely "secular," not even in Italian communes and *signorie*.[223] Nor did the Peace and Truce of God. Alfonso II's Aragonese assembly was attended not only by magnates but also by a veritable synod of bishops along with the Master of the Knights Templar, and every oath, including the king's, was sworn on the gospels. In twelfth-century Catalonia, a good many redeclarations of the Peace and Truce were made at councils in which the counts acted alongside bishops and even papal legates. The thirteenth-century *Sachsenspiegel* provided a detailed account of the customs and procedures of secular courts in Saxony; yet it still recorded the terms of the Truce of God (adding a gloss explaining why its four days were sacrosanct to Christians) and referred to "covenanted" or "bound" days (*bundenen dagen*) as days of special "peace" (*vrede*).[224]

And then there was the Languedoc. Here not only did the Peace and Truce of God continue to be an important institution; bishops continued to play the central role in its establishment and enforcement. In other words, in the region near where the Peace of God had originally developed and been strongest, it continued to develop and remain strong well into the thirteenth century. The reason for this surprising continuity is that the underlying political problems the Peace of God had been created to address had also not changed. Like Aquitaine around the year 1000, the Languedoc remained a region lacking any single, widely accepted, territorially coherent political framework. There was no Languedocian equivalent of a duke of Normandy or count of Flanders. Instead there were a number of extremely powerful seigneurial families (the most important of whom lacked even a comital title) and a welter of other lordships, all of them patchworks of districts and jurisdictional powers, none of them hegemonic in any way. The most powerful figures were the counts of Barcelona, who had begun to assert themselves across the Pyrenees in the early twelfth century; but they faced competition from the counts of Toulouse. Neither ruler had sufficiently extensive material resources in the region to build up an independent power base. Both therefore relied on alliances made individually with local lords, expressed through oaths establishing the parties' mutual rights and obligations. The result of the rivalry between Barcelona and Toulouse was the longest, most bitter series of wars in the twelfth century, as seigneurial families played each side against the other to increase their own power. No one won. No lasting, institutionally coherent principality was ever established in the Languedoc.[225]

And so as in Aquitaine in the 990s, bishops stepped into the breach. In the Languedoc and Gascony, throughout the twelfth century the Peace and Truce of God continued to be enunciated in councils held under the aegis of bishops: in Béarn and Armagnac in 1104; Toulouse in 1114;

Cahors in 1134; Périgueux between 1123 and 1137; Auch around 1140; Gascony again in 1148/49; Toulouse again around 1163; and then in and immediately after 1170 at Comminges, Rodez, Béziers, Mende, and Perpignan.[226] Save in Gascony, these remained fundamentally diocesan Peaces. The local lay nobility cooperated, but the pacts were largely arranged by bishops, and enforcement of the Peaces was organized in terms of dioceses rather than principalities. We therefore continue to find Peace militias organized by bishops within their dioceses. All males within the diocese still swore an oath to the bishop or his local curate to keep the Peace. Every oath-swearer was still required to serve in the diocesan militia when summoned to enforce the Peace against a violator.[227] The old episcopal Peace was so important in the Languedoc that new institutions were created to strengthen it. For example, to finance the Peace militias a tax was introduced to support them—the *pezade* or *commun de paix*.[228] And increasingly we find references to *paciarii* or *paziers*—judges of the Peace. It had long been a formal requirement of Peace statutes that before engaging in any act of violence to assert a legal claim in a dispute, the parties were to bring their dispute before the bishop. The *paciarii* institutionalized this requirement. Something like them are first found in the diocese of Mende in the later eleventh century, in a convention that seems to record a specific agreement between the bishop and a local lord trying to work out a concrete procedure to apply the Peace in specific cases. According to its terms, the bishop and the lord chose twenty judges (*judiciarii*) of whom twelve would hear complaints brought "according to the constitution of the peace." *Paciarii* were still a fixture at Mende and elsewhere in the Languedoc in the thirteenth century.[229] A council at Montpellier in 1215 spelled out their duties in some detail. *Paciarii* warned those who were in violation of the Peace to end their fault; they tried to end disputes before they gave rise to armed conflict; they received the persons of those arrested by lords of cities, castles, or villages for infractions of the Peace and held them until the violators had made amends for their fault. The same council also repeated the rules governing summonses of the Peace militias and required all adult males to renew their oaths of Peace every five years.[230]

The fate of the Peace and Truce of God differed in different regions, but everywhere its effects were real and lasting. In 1223 or 1224 the German king Henry VII sponsored a Peace at Würzburg in twenty-four articles. The first four articles ordained that clerics, women, nuns, peasants, merchants, hunters, fishermen, and Jews "shall have firm peace in their persons and properties"; that all churches, cemeteries, agricultural fields, mills, and settlements within their fenced or hedged boundaries "shall have the same peace"; that all highways (*strate*) shall have the peace; that one might harm one's public enemy on Mondays, Tuesdays, and Wednesdays but not on Thursdays, Fridays, Saturdays, or Sundays.[231] In France in 1155, Louis VII established "a peace for the entire kingdom" that protected all churches and their possessions, all peasants and their farming implements and animals, all merchants, and all roads.[232] In 1258 Louis IX issued a famous ordinance that outlawed all private wars (*guerras*) in the kingdom, specifically banning burnings of buildings and disturbance of peasants who used plows.[233] By the reign of Alfons II, count of Barcelona, king of Aragon, and marquis of Provence (1162–96), the laws of the court of Barcelona had been written down in the *Usatges de Barcelona*, the earliest comprehensive statement of secular legal custom in continental Europe. In several crucial passages the *Usatges* refers to "the peace and truce." Normally the phrase denotes the prince's peace and truce, but his peace and truce were still wrapped around the Peace and Truce of God. As one of the oldest articles incorporated into the collection has it:

> That rulers shall confirm and maintain for all time the peace and truce of the Lord, and act to have it confirmed and maintained by the magnates and knights of the land, as well as all men living in their country. And if anyone violates the peace and truce of the Lord in any way, he must make restitution according to the judgment of the bishops.[234]

The Peace of God became the peace of the prince. It became a commune. It even became a tax. But its core elements remained fundamentally intact, like a strand of DNA replicating across generations, gathering mutations and folded into more complex organisms but still recognizably distinct and essential.

Notes

[154] MGH Const. 1, no. 74, pp. 125–26 (Mainz).

[155] Barthélemy, *L'An mil*; Bisson, "The Organized Peace"; Hoffmann, *Gottesfriede*.

[156] Bisson, "The Organized Peace," p. 295.

[157] *Conciliorum oecumenicorum generaliumque decreta, editio critica II/1. The General councils of Latin Christendom from Constantinople IV to Pavia-Siena (869–1424)*, ed. A. García y García et al. (Turnhout: Brepols, 2013), pp. 80, 90–93, 99, 107–09, 142–43; Carraz, "Un *revival* de la paix?," p. 528. Graboïs states that Ivo of Chartres included the Peace and Truce in his *Panormia* ("De la paix de Dieu," pp. 586–87), but the pseudo-canon at issue appears to have been a conflation of decrees of Lateran II and III incorporated into late manuscripts of the *Panormia*. See the online edition by Bruce Brasington and Martin Brett at https://ivo-of-chartres.github.io/panormia.html (accessed June 2017).

[158] Vermeesch, *Essai*, pp. 57–68.

[159] Rodulfus Glaber, 4.16, pp. 196–97; Head, "The Development," p. 680 n. 114; Mansi, 19:267–68, c. 1.

[160] Van Meter, "The Peace of Amiens-Corbie"; Morelle, "La réécriture de la 'Vita Adalhardi.'"

[161] Hoffmann, *Gottesfriede*, pp. 93–97; Élisabeth Magnou-Nortier, *La Société laïque et l'église dans la province ecclésiastique de Narbonne (zone cispyrénéenne) de la fin du VIIIe à la fin du XIe siècle* (Toulouse: Association des publications de l'Université de Toulouse-Le Mirail, 1974), pp. 306–8; Barthélemy, *L'An mil*, pp. 506–13; Mansi, 19:599–604, 827–32.

[162] Hoffmann, *Gottesfriede*, pp. 166–70; Barthélemy, *L'An mil*, pp. 528–34; Barthélemy, "The Peace of God and Bishops at War in the Gallic Lands from the Late Tenth to the Early Twelfth Century," *Anglo-Norman Studies* 32 (2009): 1–23 at 17; Michel de Boüard, "Sur les origines de la Trêve de Dieu en Normandie," *Annales de Normandie* 9 (1959): 169–89.

[163] MGH Const. 1, no. 423, p. 616 n. 3; Hoffmann, *Gottesfriede*, pp. 143–48; Roger Bonnaud-Delamare, "La paix en Flandre pendant la première croisade," *Revue du Nord* 39 (1957): 147–52 (to be used with caution). For the date of Douai, see Van Meter, "The Peace of Amiens-Corbie."

[164] Bessin, p. 39.

[165] Above, pp. 47–48.

[166] *Constitucions*, nos. 1–2.

[167] Geoffrey Koziol, "Monks, Feuds, and the Making of Peace in Eleventh-Century Flanders," in *The Peace of God*, ed. Head and Landes, pp. 239–58.

[168] *GEC*, 3.53, pp. 486–87; Janssens, "La Paix de Dieu"; Van Meter, "The Peace of Amiens-Corbie"; Barthélemy, *L'An mil*, pp. 439–68.

[169] Hugh of Flavigny, *Chronicon*, 3.30, MGH SS 8:403; Barthélemy, *L'An mil*, pp. 521–23, who relies on Raoul Glaber's less well informed account.

[170] *Le registre de Lambert évêque d'Arras (1093–1115)*, ed. and trans. Claire Giordanengo (Paris: CNRS, 2007), E. 30, pp. 370–71, E. 39, pp. 380–83.

[171] Ivo of Chartres, *Epistolae*, PL 162, no. 44 (cols. 55–57); cf. also nos. 28 (cols. 40–41), 50 (61–62), 61 (75–76), 86 (107), 90 (111–12), 168 (170–72), 171 (174–75), 179 (180–81), 253 (258–59), 264 (268–69), 266 (270–71), 275 (277–78).

[172] Geoffrey Koziol, *Begging Pardon and Favor: Ritual and Political Order in Early Medieval France* (Ithaca: Cornell University Press, 1992), pp. 127–37.

[173] Vermeesch, *Essai*, pp. 60–66, c. 1.

[174] *Constitucions*, nos. 3 (Vic, 1033), 4 (Barcelona, 1064), 5 (Vic and Girona, 1064–66), 6, c. 12 , p. 12 (Toulouges, 1064–66), 7 (Girona); *HL* 5:442–45 (Toulouges, c. 1041); Bonnaud-Delamare, "Les institutions de paix" (Douai, Thérouanne); Fortunier and Pericard, "Odilon," pp. 131–33 (Arles) (above, chap. 2, n. 139); Bessin, p. 39 (Caen); Mansi, 19:827–32, c. 5 (Narbonne); Vermeesch, *Essai*, pp. 59–66, c. 9 (Saint-Omer).

[175] *Constitucions*, no. 4, c. 15. This was probably implicit in other Catalan Peaces, which required payment of compensation for all violations of the Truce.

[176] MGH Const. 1, no. 422, c. 2, pp. 599–601.

[177] *Constitucions*, no. 4, cc. 11, 14, pp. 15–16 (Barcelona, 1064), no. 5, cc. 4, 6, 14, pp. 23–24 (Vic and Girona, 1064–66). Narbonne in 1054 awarded double compensation to the injured party: Mansi, 19:832, c. 26.

[178] Vermeesch, *Essai*, p. 64, c. 10 (Soissons); also a related Peace from Arras, cited by Bonnaud-Delamare, "La paix en Flandre," p. 150 (above, n. 163).

[179] Vermeesch, *Essai*, p. 64, c. 10 (Soissons, Saint-Omer).

[180] Koziol, *Begging Pardon*, chap. 7 (above, n. 172).

[181] Bonnaud-Delamare, "Les institutions de paix," pp. 152, 184 bis.

[182] Vermeesch, *Essai*, pp. 64–65.

[183] Bisson, "The Organized Peace," p. 294.

[184] Bessin, p. 39 (Caen, 1040s); MGH Const. 1, no. 422, p. 600 (Thérouanne, c. 1060); cf. Goetz, "Die Kölner Gottesfriede," pp. 42–43, 64.

[185] Orderic Vitalis, 5.5, 3:24–37.

[186] Vermeesch, *Essai*, pp. 59–66.

[187] Fernand Vercauteren, *Actes des comtes de Flandre (1071–1128)* (Brussels: Palais des Académies, 1938), pp. xxxviii (no. 18), xlii (no. 30), no. 49, pp. 125–26, no. 53, pp. 133–34, no. 65, pp. 153–55; MGH Const. 1, no. 432, pp. 616–17 with p. 616 n. 3; Hoffmann, *Gottesfriede*, pp. 144, 151–53.

[188] MGH Const. 1, no. 432, pp. 616–17.

[189] MGH Const. 1, no. 432, pp. 616–17 n. 3.

[190] Reading *herilis* as *herisliz* (to lay down arms after a campaign).

[191] *La paix de Valenciennes de 1114*, ed. Philippe Godding and J. Pycke (Louvain-la-Neuve: Institut d'études médiévales, 1981), p. 29 and n. 90.

[192] Ibid., pp. 99–137, especially cc. 1–2, 4, 13–14, 42–44.

[193] For example, Orderic Vitalis, 11.11, 6:62–69.

[194] Galbert of Bruges, *Histoire du meurtre de Charles le Bon, comte de Flandre (1127–1128)*, ed. Henri Pirenne (Paris, 1891), cc. 33 (the militia of Ghent being referred to as a *communio*), 51, 53, 55, 72, 93–99, 103, 106.

[195] Vermeesch, *Essai*, pp. 88–116; Achille Luchaire, *Louis VI le Gros: Annales de sa vie et de son règne (1081–1137)* (Paris, 1890), pp. cxcii–cxciii.

[196] *Actus pontificum Cenomannis in urbe degentium*, ed. G. Busson and A. Ledru, Archives historiques du Maine 2 (Le Mans: Société des Archives historiques du Maine, 1901), pp. 376–80; Vermeesch, *Essai*, pp. 81–87.

[197] Orderic Vitalis, 9.3, 5:20–21.

[198] Vermeesch, *Essai*, pp. 62–63.

[199] Hugh of Flavigny, *Chronicon*, MGH SS 8:477–78; Vermeesch, *Essai*, pp. 69–70.

[200] William Mendel Newman, *Le domaine royal sous les premiers Capétiens (987–1180)* (Paris: Librairie du Recueil Sirey, 1937).

[201] Orderic Vitalis, 8.24, 4:286–89.

[202] Orderic Vitalis, 11.34, 6:156–57.

[203] Orderic Vitalis, 11.19, 6:244–45. For these and other examples, see Vermeesch, *Essai*, pp. 72–73, 113–16; Julia Exarchos, "Louis VI, the Bishop of Arras, and Royal Empowerment: Scripting Liturgy of War in Early Twelfth-Century France," forthcoming; Graboïs, "De la trêve de Dieu."

[204] Suger of Saint-Denis, *La geste de Louis VI*, ed. Michel Bur (Paris: Imprimerie nationale, 1994), c. 16; cf. Graboïs, "De la paix de Dieu."

[205] Vermeesch, *Essai*, pp. 113–16; Graboïs, "De la paix de Dieu," p. 588, suggests 1111.

[206] Graboïs, "De la paix de Dieu," pp. 588–89; Suger, *La Geste de Louis VI*, c. 24 (above, n. 204).

[207] For what follows, see especially Wadle, *Landfrieden*. A good brief survey, somewhat traditionally legalistic, is given by Karl Kroeschell, *Deutsche Rechtsgeschichte*, vol. 1 (Oplanden, 1980), pp. 184–98; vol. 2 (Oplanden, 1980), pp. 159–61. In English, the only good treatment is Alan Harding, *Medieval Law and the Foundations of the State* (Oxford: Oxford University Press, 2002), pp. 79–98.

[208] MGH SS 25:90, 131 (Liège); MGH Const. 1, no. 424, pp. 602–05 (Cologne); H. Vander Linden, "Le tribunal de la paix de Henri de Verdun (1082) et la formation de la principauté de Liège," in *Mélanges d'histoire offerts à Henri Pirenne*, vol. 2 (Brussels: Vromant, 1926), pp. 589–96; Goetz, "Der Kölner Gottesfriede."

[209] MGH Const. 1, nos. 74, pp. 125–26 (Mainz 1103), 425, pp. 605–08 (Mainz 1085), 426, pp. 608–09 (Goslar); MGH SS 6:227 (Nordhausen).

[210] MGH Const. 1, nos. 140, pp. 194–98 (1152), 176, pp. 245–47 (1158), 277, pp. 380–83 (1179).

[211] MGH Const. 2, nos. 196, pp. 241–63 (1235), 319, pp. 428–29 (1234).

[212] *The Saxon Mirror: A Sachsenspiegel of the Fourteenth Century*, trans. Maria Dobozy (Philadelphia: University of Pennsylvania Press, 1999), pp. 43–50.

[213] MGH Const. 1, no. 427, p. 610.

[214] MGH Const. 1, nos. 427, pp. 609–10 (Bavaria), 429, pp. 611–13 (Alsace); MGH Const. 2, no. 425, pp. 566–68 (Hainaut); Gottfried Partsch, "Ein unbekannter Walliser Landfrieden aus dem 12. Jahrhundert," *Zeitschrift der Savigny-Stiftung für Rechtsgeschichte, Germanistische Abteilung* 75 (1958): 94–107 (Valais).

[215] Elmar Wadle, "Landfriedensrecht in der Praxis," in *Landfrieden: Anspruch und Wirklichkeit*, ed. Arno Buschmann and Elmar Wadle, Veröffentlichungen der Görres-Gesellschaft, NF 98 (Paderborn: Schöningh, 2002), pp. 73–94 at 86–87.

[216] Hartmut Boockmann, "Landfriedensbestimmungen aus dem Sachsenspiegel," *Geschichte in Wissenschaft und Unterricht* 50 (1999): 163–70.

[217] *Constitucions*, nos. 2–3, pp. 6–7, 8–11.

[218] *Constitucions*, no. 4, pp. 12–19.

[219] *Constitucions*, no. 5, pp. 20–28, no. 6, pp. 29–35. For the Catalan counties see Stephen P. Bensch, "La séparation des comtés d'Empúries et du Roussillon," *Annales du Midi* 118 (2006): 405–10.

[220] *Constitucions*, no. 8, pp. 40–42.

[221] *Constitucions*, no. 9, pp. 43–44.

[222] *Colección de documentos inéditos del Archivo general de la Corona de Aragón*, ed. Próspero de Bofarull y Mascaró, vol. 8 (Barcelona, 1847–1973), pp. 36–41.

[223] Augustine Thompson, *Cities of God: The Religion of the Italian Communes, 1125–1325* (University Park: Pennsylvania State University Press, 2005).

[224] *Sachsenspiegel: Landrecht*, ed. K. A. Eckhardt, 2nd ed., MGH Fontes iuris Germanici, n.s. 1.1 (Göttingen: Musterschmidt-Verlag, 1955), 2.10, p. 135.

[225] Débax, *La Féodalité languedocienne*; Hélène Couderc-Barraud, *La Violence, l'ordre et la paix: Résoudre les conflits en Gascogne du XIᵉ au début du XIIIᵉ siècle* (Toulouse: Presses universitaire du Mirail, 2008).

[226] For these councils see Bisson, "The Organized Peace," and Carraz, "Un *revival* de la paix?"

[227] Jean-Louis Biget, "L'épiscopat du Rouergue et de l'Albigeois (Xᵉ–XIᵉ siècle)," in *Catalunya i França Meridional a l'entorn de l'any mil / La Catalogne et la France méridionale autour de l'an mil, Barcelona, 2–5 juliol 1987*, ed. Xavier Barral i Altet et al. (Barcelona, 1991), pp. 181–99 at 192–94; Brunel, "Juges de paix," pp. 34–38; Couderc-Barraud, *La violence*, p. 122 (above, n. 225); Vermeesch, *Essai*, pp. 48–57.

[228] Bisson, "The Organized Peace," pp. 297–302; Frédéric Boutoulle, "La paix et la trêve de Dieu du Liber rubeus," in *L'Église et la société dans le diocèse de Dax aux XIᵉ et XIIᵉ siècles. Journée d'études sur le "Livre rouge" de la cathédrale de Dax, Dax, 1ᵉʳ mai 2003*, ed. Jean Cabanot and Jean-Bernard Marquette (Dax: Comité d'études sur l'histoire et l'art de la Gascogne, 2004), pp. 47–72 at 54–60; Carraz, "*Sub eiusdem pacis*," pp. 25–30; Carraz, "Un *revival* de la paix?," pp. 532–34.

[229] Bisson, "The Organized Peace"; Brunel, "Les juges de paix"; Carraz, "*Sub eiusdem pacis*."

[230] Mansi, 22:935–54, cc. 32–39.

[231] MGH Const. 2, no. 284, pp. 398–401, cc. 1–4.

[232] *RHF* 14:387; Graboïs, "De la paix de Dieu."

[233] *Ordonnances*, 1:84; Justine Firnhaber-Baker, "From God's Peace to the King's Order: Late Medieval Limitations on Non-Royal Warfare," *Essays in Medieval Studies* 23 (2006): 19–30.

[234] *The Usatges of Barcelona: The Fundamental Law of Catalonia*, trans. Donald J. Kagay (Philadelphia: University of Pennsylvania Press, 1994), c. 78; cf. cc. 57–62, 71, 74, 78, 124.

Conclusion

Aware of the many flaws in the idea of a sudden "feudal mutation" around the turn of the millennium, Thomas Bisson proposed instead a "crisis of lordship."[235] The difficulty is that his crisis lasted for some 350 years, too long a time for the idea of "crisis" to be meaningful. What if we spoke instead of the "problem" of lordship? This might be more useful, because it calls attention to the very issue that critics of a "feudal mutation" have insisted on: most of the developments adduced as signs of a mutation in the decades surrounding the millennium actually appeared well before 900. That is when we find increasing evidence of the powerful controlling the labour of dependent peasants on estates in ways so systematic that in aggregate it constitutes a new mode of production. It is when we begin to find fortifications constructed not by kings against Viking raiders but as military structures built by the locally powerful to hold territory against rivals. The garrisons manning those castles and the military expeditions launched from them required provisions; so this was also the time when we find references to "customs" that were really exactions for military requisitions levied in excess from peasants. In other words, the second half of the ninth century saw the creation of the foundations of what we think of as "lordship." It was also when, out of the many Carolingian usages of "peace," Hincmar of Reims seized on one called "the peace of the army" that prohibited unlawful military requisitions. Hincmar described such requisitions as acts of *violentia, depraedatio, raptio*—the very language that would later be applied by the Peace of God to very similar actions. The reason historians can argue that the Peace of God was essentially Carolingian is because the kind of lordship addressed by the Peace was, in its fundamental structures, a development of the late Carolingian period in the West Frankish kingdom.

It was also in the later ninth century and in the same kingdom that we begin to find a propensity to the fragmentation of political authority. At first, this did not pose a problem locally, since the great princes were able to maintain order within their territories. By the later tenth century that was no longer the case. Castles were everywhere, as were lordships. And the lordships were not territorially distinct and coherent. Lordship was not yet a territory; it was a power, the exercise of certain kinds of rights (military, judicial, and fiscal), with different rights asserted over the same lands and people by different lords (and different kinds of lords, from counts and viscounts to castellans and advocates to bishops, cathedral chapters, and monasteries). And the period's legal norms did not just allow violence in prosecuting disputes, they actively promoted it by requiring the public exercise of a right in order to claim it, and the public resistance to such actions in order to deny it. Making this problem worse was another: the erosion of coherent, inclusive political frameworks within which disputes between lords could be resolved. The problem was worst in Aquitaine and the Languedoc after the failure of once powerful princely houses, but it could appear elsewhere as well: whenever a minority unleashed a spate of *werrae*; whenever a region of lordships was taken over by an outside prince; whenever two outside powers contended for control of a territory.

In these circumstances bishops were able to fill the political vacuum. By kinship they were the close relatives of the regional nobility. As lords themselves they commanded their own warriors and ruled their own lands and peasants. But their ecclesiastical office also made them "judges of peace" who privileged negotiation and compromise in trying to end conflicts. They were also beneficiaries of a long tradition of law and legislation, much of which concerned the protection of ecclesiastical lands and persons, the protection of the weak, and the proper uses of excommunication and anathema. Just as important, the episcopal tradition was a conciliar tradition. Bishops were used to meeting in councils—both diocesan councils and provincial councils. And since they were kinsmen of princes and lords of lands and warriors, they were used to bringing lay elites into their governance. In the absence of any recognized secular venue for resolving disputes between lords over the fundamental rights of lordship, episcopal councils provided a suitable forum for meetings and discussions. There bishops could gather with abbots and monks and lords great and small, and all could deliberate together about *werrae*. The result was legislation, but not legislation as the Carolingians had practiced it— fervent, ideological, and utterly unpragmatic. The legislation of the Peace councils resulted from negotiation, compromise, and consent. The Peace of God did not promote an ideal peace like Alcuin's, nor an ideological peace like Hincmar's. It promoted a peace that was the best one could achieve under the circumstances, a peace full of conditions, qualifications, and exceptions. But then, this was the very oldest legal definition of a peace, of a "pact": a qualification and condition stipulated by the agreement of two parties that amended the law without violating it, and thereby adapted the law to their specific needs. In the tenth and eleventh centuries, this remained one of the most common definitions of a peace, as illustrated by any number of charters recording sales, donations, and exchanges and introducing specific stipulations with the connective, *eo pacto* ....

The legislation of the Peace of God proved so useful that within just two decades a consistent *forma pacis* had developed that spread throughout the entirety of the old West Frankish kingdom, from Barcelona to Saint-Omer. The reason for its success was that it did not even try to outlaw lordship and violence. It codified them. It allowed lords to do pretty much everything lords wanted to do with their own peasants—including beat them, seize their persons for perceived misdeeds, take their belongings for redemption—as long as they did not do the same with peasants who were not their dependents or whose dependency was itself in dispute. It allowed lords to build castles but restricted when the castles could be built, and under certain conditions required notification of their building. It allowed lords to fortify churches as long as they did not use the fortifications as a base for military expeditions. It allowed lords to take requisitions for military expeditions, but no more than what was due them. It allowed lords on military expeditions to attack those who were their armed enemies but not defenceless neutrals who were unarmed, nor the animals needed by peasants, nor the merchandise needed by traders. It assumed that disputes might end in a *werra*, but it required a preliminary effort to settle the issues peacefully before a count and bishop. And in the end, it allowed legitimate *werrae* against those lords and their supporters who violated these agreed-upon terms.

The Peace of God was not really peace at all. It was Europe's first true legislation and its first law of war. That is why it was important.

Notes

[235] Thomas N. Bisson, *The Crisis of the Twelfth Century: Power, Lordship, and the Origins of European Government* (Princeton: Princeton University Press, 2009).

Further Reading

Barthélemy, Dominique. *L'An mil et la paix de Dieu: La France chrétienne et féodale, 980–1060*. Paris: Fayard, 1999.

> Comprehensive, detailed, and always smart, with many full (French) translations of Latin sources, but idiosyncratic and underfootnoted. Especially good, however, on the Peace of Vienne and its important derivatives.

Bisson, Thomas N. "The Organized Peace in Southern France and Catalonia, ca. 1140–ca. 1233." *American Historical Review* 82 (1977): 290–311.

> Dense and difficult but fundamental on the later institutionalization of the southern Peace and Truce.

Bonnaud-Delamare, Roger. *L'idée de paix à l'époque carolingienne*. Paris: Domat-Montchrestien, 1939.

> As in most of his work, the author's interpretation is quite dated, here in thrall to a false interpretation of early medieval ideas about peace as fundamentally Augustinian; yet the book contains a wealth of useful references to important sources.

———. "Les institutions de paix dans la province ecclési-astique de Reims au XIᵉ siècle." *Bulletin philologique et historique du Comité des travaux historiques et scien-tifiques* (1957): 143–200.

> The first close analysis of the Peace texts now often grouped under their incipit "Fratres karissimi," and still important as orientation to the Peace in northern France.

Brunel, Clovis. "Les juges de la paix en Gévaudan au milieu du XIᵉ siècle." *Bibliothèque de l'École des Chartes* 109 (1951): 32–41.

> A cogently argued exposition of Peace institutions in south-ern France.

Carraz, Damien. "Un *revival* de la paix de Dieu? Les paix diocésaines du XIIᵉ siècle dans le Midi." In *La réforme "gré-gorienne" dans le Midi*, pp. 523–58. Cahiers de Fanjeaux 48. Toulouse: Privat, 2013.

> A good, if broad, history of the institutionalization of the Peace in Gascony and the Languedoc.

———. "*Sub eiusdem pacis et treugue dei defensione*: Die Ritterorden und der Frieden in Südfrankreich im 12. Jahrhundert." *Ordines militares* 17 (2012): 17–39.

> A fascinating study of the institutionalization of the Peace in southern France, focussing on the role of the Templars and Hospitallers in collecting peace-taxes and establishing *salva-menta* subject to peace regulations.

Débax, Hélène. *La Féodalité languedocienne, XIᵉ–XIIᵉ siè-cles: Serments, hommages et fiefs dans le Languedoc des Trencavel*. Toulouse: Université de Toulouse-Le Mirail, 2003.

> Though not on the Peace, this is a superb study of Langue-docian politics in the twelfth century that provides essential context and an especially good treatment of *convenientiae*.

Gergen, Thomas. *Pratique juridique de la paix et trêve de Dieu à partir du concile de Charroux (989-1250) / Juristische Praxis der Pax und Treuga Dei ausgehend vom Konzil von Charroux (989-1250).* Rechtshistorische Reihe 285. Frankfurt am Main: Peter Lang, 2003.

> Unnecessarily repetitive and myopically focused on the Peace as legislation to the exclusion of all other elements; yet much of the argument has great merit.

Goetz, Hans-Werner. "Kirchenschutz, Rechtswahrung und Reform: Zu den Zielen und zum Wesen der frühen Gottesfriedensbewegung in Frankreich." *Francia* 11 (1983): 193-239.

> The best short article on the early Peace and Truce, with full references to primary sources and judicious discussions of political, cultural, and religious contexts. A highly abridged version is translated in *The Peace of God*, ed. Head and Landes.

———. "Der Kölner Gottesfriede von 1083: Beobachtungen über Anfänge, Tradition und Eigenart der deutschen Gottesfriedensbewegung." *Jahrbuch des Kölnischen Geschichtsverein* 55 (1984): 39-76.

> Convincingly establishes that the German *Landfriede* originated in the Peace of God.

Graboïs, Aryeh. "De la trêve de Dieu à la paix du roi: étude sur les transformations du mouvement de la paix au XIIᵉ siècle." In *Mélanges offerts à René Crozet à l'occasion de son 70ᵉ anniversaire par ses amis, ses collègues, ses élèves et les membres du C.E.S.C.M.* 2 vols. Poitiers, 1966.

> Although dated in both its model of political authority and its scholarship, provides a good, short statement of the traditional view and identifies some crucial moments of change.

Guillot, Olivier. "Formes, fondements et limites de l'organisation politique en France au Xe s." In *Il secolo di ferro: Mito e realità del secolo X, 19-25 aprile 1990*, 1:57-124. Settimane di studio del Centro italiano di studi sull'alto medioevo 38:1-2. Spoleto: Centro italiano di studi sull'alto medioevo, 1991.

> Brief but sophisticated, far and away the best short analysis of tenth-century West Frankish high politics.

Head, Thomas. "The Development of the Peace of God in Aquitaine (970–1005)." *Speculum* 74 (1999): 656-86.

> The fruit of long work on the early Peace councils, and crammed full of important details on their political context and participants.

Hoffmann, Hartmut. *Gottesfriede und Treuga Dei*. MGH Schriften 20. Stuttgart: A. Hiersemann, 1964.

> Still the most useful and comprehensive history of the movement, with full discussions of all primary sources for each instantiation.

Janssens, Sam. "La Paix de Dieu dans les *Gesta episcoporum Cameracensium*." *Revue du Nord* 97 (2015): 301-16.

> A clear discussion of one of the most problematic sources on the Peace.

Jégou, Laurent. *L'évêque, juge de paix: L'autorité épiscopale et le règlement des conflits (VIIIe–XIe siècle)*. Turnhout: Brepols, 2011.

> Though not on the Peace of God, essential to understanding the episcopate's overdetermined investment in peace-making.

Jones, Anna Trumbore. *Noble Lord, Good Shepherd: Episcopal Power and Piety in Aquitaine, 877-1050*. Leiden: Brill, 2009.

> Provides excellent background on the political, religious, and familial aims of the Aquitainian bishops who originated the Peace of God.

Kosto, Adam J. "The *Convenientia* in the Early Middle Ages." *Mediaeval Studies* 60 (1998): 1-54.

> If one were to read just one piece of scholarship on the vexed question of *convenientiae*, this would be it.

Koziol, Geoffrey. "The Conquest of Burgundy, the Peace of God, and the Diplomas of Robert the Pious." *French Historical Studies* 37 (2014): 173-214.

> A thorough reconsideration of the Burgundian Peace councils and their role in Robert the Pious's takeover of Burgundy.

Magnou-Nortier, Élisabeth. "The Enemies of the Peace: Reflections on a Vocabulary, 500-1100." In *The Peace of God*, ed. Head and Landes, pp. 58-79.

——. "Les évêques et la paix dans l'espace franc (VIe-XIe siècles)." In *L'Évêque dans l'histoire de l'église*, pp. 33-50. Angers: Presses de l'Université d'Angers, 1984.

——. "Les mauvaises coutumes en Auvergne, Bourgogne méridionale, Languedoc et Provence au XIe siècle: un moyen d'analyse sociale." In *Structures féodales et féodalisme dans l'Occident méditerranéen (Xe-XIIIe siècles): Bilan et perspectives de recherches*, pp. 135-72. Collection de l'École française de Rome 44. Rome: École française de Rome, 1980.

————. "La place du Concile du Puy (v. 994) dans l'évolution de l'idée de paix." In *Mélanges offerts à Jean Dauvillier*, pp. 489–506. Toulouse: Centre d'histoire juridique méridionale, 1979.

> Magnou-Nortier is always fascinating to read, even if her conclusions are problematic, given her uncompromising commitment to a model of institutional continuity throughout the early Middle Ages.

Morelle, Laurent. "La réécriture de la 'Vita Adalhardi' de Paschase Radbert au XIe siècle: auteur, date et context." In *Amicorum societas: Mélanges offerts à François Dolbeau pour son 65e anniversaire*, pp. 485–99. Florence: SISMEL, 2013.

> A rigorous analysis of the major sources for the various Peaces of Amiens and Corbie that clarifies their dates, contexts, and purposes.

The Peace of God: Social Violence and Religious Response in France around the Year 1000. Edited by Thomas Head and Richard Landes. Ithaca: Cornell University Press, 1992.

> For a long time the only good English-language overview of the Peace. However, many of the contributors' conclusions assume a "feudal mutation" that most scholars now doubt. Frederick Paxton's essay on the historiography of the Peace remains extremely valuable.

Riches, Theo. "The Peace of God, the 'Weakness' of Robert the Pious and the Struggle for the German Throne, 1023–5." *Early Medieval Europe* 18 (2010): 202–22.

> A fine, thorough analysis of the politics underlying Gerard of Cambrai's hostility to the Peace.

Van Meter, David C. "The Peace of Amiens-Corbie and Gerard of Cambrai's Oration on the Three Functional Orders: The Date, the Context, the Rhetoric." *Revue belge de philologie et d'histoire* 74 (1996): 633–57.

A well-reasoned investigation of the rationale behind Gerard of Cambrai's criticisms of the Peace of God that also establishes the date of the first Peace of Amiens-Corbie.

Vermeesch, Albert. *Essai sur les origines et la signification de la commune dans le nord de la France (XIe et XIIe siècles)*. Heule: UGA, 1966.

The classic work showing the links between the Peace and early communes.

Wadle, Elmar. *Landfrieden, Strafe, Recht: Zwölf Studien zum Mittelalter*. Schriften zur Europäischen Rechts- und Verfassungsgeschichte 37. Berlin: Duncker & Humblot, 2001.

The single best introduction to the German *Landfriede*.

Printed and bound by CPI Group (UK) Ltd, Croydon, CR0 4YY

12/06/2024

14514398-0003